Measurement of Nontariff Barriers

SIE *Studies in International Economics* includes works dealing with the theory; empirical analysis; political, economic, and legal aspects; and evaluation of international policies and institutions.

Keith E. Maskus, Peter M. Hooper, Edward E. Leamer, and J. David Richardson, Editors
Quiet Pioneering: Robert M. Stern and His International Economic Legacy

Bjarne S. Jensen and Kar-yiu Wong, Editors
Dynamics, Economic Growth, and International Trade

Kala Marathe Krishna and Ling Hui Tan
Rags and Riches: Implementing Apparel Quotas under the Multi-Fibre Arrangement

Alan V. Deardorff and Robert M. Stern
Measurement of Nontariff Barriers

Thomas Cottier and Petros C. Mavroidis, Editors
The World Trade Forum, Volume I: State Trading in the Twenty-First Century

Rajesh Chadha, Sanjib Pohit, Alan V. Deardorff, and Robert M. Stern
The Impact of Trade and Domestic Policy Reforms in India: A CGE Modeling Approach

Alan V. Deardorff and Robert M. Stern, Editors
Constituent Interests and U.S. Trade Policies

Gary R. Saxonhouse and T. N. Srinivasan, Editors
Development, Duality, and the International Economic Regime: Essays in Honor of Gustav Ranis

Measurement of Nontariff Barriers

Alan V. Deardorff and Robert M. Stern

Ann Arbor

THE UNIVERSITY OF MICHIGAN PRESS

Published in the United States of America by
The University of Michigan Press
Manufactured in the United States of America
♾ Printed on acid-free paper

2001 2000 1999 1998 4 3 2 1

A CIP catalog record for this book is available from the British Library.

Library of Congress Cataloging-in-Publication Data

Deardorff, Alan V.
Measurement of nontariff barriers / Alan V. Deardorff and Robert M. Stern.
p. cm. — (Studies in international economics)
Includes bibliographical references and index.
ISBN 0-472-10931-6 (cloth : alk. paper)
1. Nontariff trade barriers—Statistical methods. I. Stern, Robert Mitchell, 1927– . II. Measurement of non-tariff barriers. III. Title. IV. Series: Studies in international economics (Ann Arbor, Mich.)
HF1430.D428 1999
382′.3—dc21 98-46620
CIP

Contents

Preface

This book is a revised and extended version of a study of the measurement of nontariff barriers (NTBs) that was commissioned in December 1995 by the Economics Department of the Organisation for Economic Co-Operation and Development (OECD). An earlier version of this study was issued as Economics Department Working Paper No. 179 by the OECD in 1997.

The terms of reference for the study were as follows:

> "The main objective of the OECD pilot group (PG) is to evaluate the usefulness and improve the accuracy of methods for quantifying non-tariff border measures (NTBs), and encourage wider efforts to quantify the effects of NTBs within member countries. The commissioned report under these terms of reference would:
>
> - assess currently available methods for quantifying NTBs, and make recommendations as to those that can be most effectively employed;
> - evaluate the work of the pilot group members and others in quantifying individual and nation-wide NTBs;
> - provide a rough assessment of the importance of currently-employed NTBs as measures to shift the allocation of resources; and
> - provide a guide to methods that countries could apply in quantifying the effects of their own NTBs.
>
> Thus, the report would assess both the importance and the current success of efforts to quantify NTBs, and provide guidelines to governments and researchers who may wish to quantify various NTBs. The guidelines would relate both to the choice between alternative methodologies and the implementation of these methodologies (e.g., data requirements)."

We were attracted to undertake this study especially because it gave us the opportunity to return to the subject of NTBs that we had addressed in our earlier and widely cited 1985 study conducted for the United Nations Conference on Trade and Development (UNCTAD), *Methods of Measurement of Non-Tariff Barriers*. We make frequent reference to our UNCTAD study in the chapters that follow in the present work.

In carrying out the present study, we would like to thank Michael Daly, Ketil Hviding, and Nicholas Vanston of the OECD Economics Department for their assistance in providing us with materials prepared by the OECD IGA Pilot Group. We also wish to acknowledge the many helpful comments on earlier versions of this study that we received from members of the Pilot Group that consisted of representatives from Australia, Canada, Germany, Norway, United Kingdom, and the United States and from the World Trade Organization (WTO) and OECD staffs. Bernard Hoekman also provided a number of useful comments in various phases of the study. Useful comments were provided as well by two anonymous external reviewers who were commissioned to evaluate the manuscript for the University of Michigan Press.

We owe special thanks to Judith Jackson for her exceptionally able and patient effort in helping to prepare and edit the manuscript and for adapting it for camera-ready format for purposes of publication. We are grateful also to Ellen McCarthy, Economics Editor of the University of Michigan Press, for her assistance in shepherding the manuscript through the various stages of the publication process.

Alan V. Deardorff
Robert M. Stern

Tables

CHAPTER 1

Introduction

Because tariffs on imports of manufactures have been reduced to relatively low levels in the major industrialized countries especially as the result of the periodic rounds of multilateral trade negotiations, there has been increasing interest in the extent to which existing nontariff barriers (NTBs) may distort and restrict international trade. In order to address the issues involving the use and impacts of NTBs, it is self-evident that accurate and reliable measures are needed. In this study, we will assess currently available methods for quantifying NTBs and make recommendations as to those methods that can be most effectively employed. We will focus both on the conceptual issues arising in the measurement of the different types of NTBs and on the applied research that has been carried out in studies prepared by country members of the OECD Pilot Group and others seeking to quantify NTBs.

In considering NTBs, it is interesting to ask why governments may prefer them to tariffs. While there may not be a single answer to this, Deardorff (1987) suggests some possible explanations. These include: institutional constraints such as are built into the GATT/WTO rules and into national constitutions that limit the use of tariffs; the roles of firms and workers in influencing the choice of policies; considerations of reaction to or retaliation against the policies of trading partners; and uncertainty about the ways in which different policies may perform. Deardorff favors the last of these explanations insofar as governments perceive that tariffs will not work effectively in reducing imports. That is, if the object is to assist firms and workers who purportedly are being injured by imports, he shows that only an explicit quantitative (nontariff) restriction can be relied on to do the job in an uncertain world. In any event, whatever the motivations of governments may be, we will take the presence of NTBs for granted and not try to determine the circumstances in which they are in fact used.

In what follows, we present in chapter 2 a typology of NTBs, and we discuss some of their salient economic characteristics. Chapter 3 considers the conceptual aspects and selected applications of *general* methods for measuring the presence and size of NTBs, as well as *special purpose* and *specific* methods that are applicable to the most commonly used NTBs. In chapter 4, we provide an overview and assessment of the methods and numerical results of the measurement of NTBs drawn mainly from the OECD Pilot Group studies, and we highlight the major lessons to be drawn from these studies. This should be viewed as only a sampling of the empirical work that is available on NTBs, and it is by no means a comprehensive survey or review of that literature, for which we refer the reader to Laird and Yeats (1990). In chapter 5, we conclude by presenting our own guidelines for measuring NTBs, followed by detailed recommendations of procedures to be used in individual cases and under specific assumptions. An annotated listing of the major categories of NTBs and related policies is contained in appendix 1. Illustrative measures of the components of the nominal and effective rates of assistance are provided in appendix 2. Algebraic formulas pertinent to the recommended procedures for measuring particular NTBs under varying assumptions are presented and motivated in appendix 3. Barriers to trade in services and foreign direct investment are discussed briefly in appendix 4.

CHAPTER 2

Typology and Characteristics of NTBs

In this chapter we first present and discuss briefly a typology of NTBs that may exist in different countries, and thereafter we analyze some salient characteristics of NTBs. Our discussion is intended to serve as background for the chapters to follow that deal with methods of measurement of NTBs and with the OECD Pilot Group Studies.

Typology of NTBs

A basic difficulty in approaching NTBs is that they are defined by what they are not. That is, NTBs consist of all barriers to trade that are not tariffs. Indeed they are even more general than that, since the term is often used to include trade interventions such as export subsidies that serve to stimulate rather than retard trade and therefore are not "barriers" to trade at all. Thus NTBs include such well-known trade distorting policies as import quotas and voluntary export restraints (VERs). And they also include a potentially unlimited plethora of policies, perhaps as yet not invented, that alter however indirectly the prices and/or quantities of trade.

In this situation, no typology of NTBs can possibly be complete. However, to give some idea of their diversity, we provide in appendix 1 a list and brief description of the most important existing NTBs. The measures noted range from narrowly conceived ones affecting particular products, industries, and countries to more general ones that are rooted in national institutions and policies.[1] Evidently the list of NTBs is large and diverse, and, as we will note in our later discussion, it may be difficult to devise accurate measurements of many of them.

If we examine the details of appendix 1 more closely, it appears that some barriers may be formal in the sense that they are stated explicitly in official legislation or governmental mandates. But there may also be informal barriers arising from: (1) administrative procedures and unpublished government regulations and policies; (2) market structure; and (3) political, social, and cultural institutions. The impediments associated with informal barriers may be the result of a conscious effort by government to favor domestic over foreign interests, or they may be the byproduct of practices and policies that are rooted in domestic institutions. Since informal barriers may be important in their own right and pose difficult measurement problems, some comments concerning them may be useful.

Administrative Procedures and Government Regulations and Policies

It is well known that the procedures employed to administer policies and regulations could in themselves constitute impediments to trade. For example, discretionary licensing could be used in implementing import quotas or export restraints. Customs procedures may rely on specially constructed measures of price for valuation purposes and involve costly administrative protocols in order to favor domestic producers. A further example is that antidumping, countervailing duty, and other types of investigation of alleged unfair trade actions may be used to foster a climate of uncertainty for foreign suppliers and as a method of harassment designed to bring about changes in foreign trading practices and policies. Domestic regulations and policies may also result in a variety of impediments to trade, depending upon their intent and the structural changes and behavioral responses that are induced.

Market Structure

Industry market structures may range from perfectly competitive to single firm monopolies. Such differences in the degree of industry competition between nations are often perceived as creating impediments to trade. While there may be grounds for such perceptions, it is important to understand what the determinants of market structure are in given circumstances. Again, governmental policies need to be taken into account. Thus, for example, nations may differ in the extent to which they rely on public ownership, monopolization, and the regulation of economic activity. Given these differences, there are bound to be difficulties when national policies impinge on the interests of foreign producers. The issue here is closely tied in with national sovereignty and the domestic objectives that governments believe that they have the right to pursue.

A related consideration is how a government's competition/antitrust policies are designed to affect the organization and behavior of private business firms. That is, governments obviously differ in the extent to which they actively pursue policies to promote competition or condone collusive market structures. To the extent that competition is constrained, this may constitute an important informal barrier to trade. By the same token, there may be substantial benefits at home and abroad arising from more active unilateral pursuit of policies to foster competition.

Institutional Factors

A final issue is whether differences in political, social, and cultural institutions should be viewed as constituting informal barriers to trade. In a federal system, for example, the locus of economic policies may vary considerably among the central government, states or provinces, and local government. Thus, in the United States, state governments are generally not permitted to institute policies that are at variance with those of the federal government. However, conformity may not always be achieved, as witnessed by the preferential procurement policies that some U.S. states have attempted to follow. Similarly in Canada, the provinces have their own procurement policies, and there is the unusual practice that permits provincial ownership of natural resources.

Nations may differ markedly in terms of their social and cultural institutions and the policies that governments believe to be in the national interest. For example, there may be national differences in policies affecting the availability of residential housing and land, which could in turn have a significant impact on private savings behavior and the current account. The United States and Japan stand in contrast on this point. Nations may also institute policies designed to enhance their cultural identity and values. Further, consumer tastes and spending habits will be conditioned by the domestic social and cultural environment, and there may well be a reluctance to purchase foreign products that are considered inferior to their domestic counterparts. The question here is whether national differences in consumer behavior should be considered as an informal barrier to trade. It is by no means clear to us that they should.

The preceding discussion suggests that there may be a variety of informal barriers to trade arising from administrative procedures and government regulations and policies and from national differences in market structure and competition policies. As we will note below, in contrast to formal barriers to trade, informal barriers may be especially difficult to measure.

Characteristics of Nontariff Barriers

In view of the vast array of formal and/or informal NTBs that may exist, there may not be a single analytical methodology capable of dealing completely with the entire spectrum of NTBs. Yet, if we can identify those aspects of the effects that are cause for concern, it is conceivable that a single technique could measure one of these effects quite comprehensively. Thus, it is essential that we approach the question of measuring NTBs, which is the subject of chapter 3 below, by first looking at their potentially measurable effects.[2]

A start towards an understanding of NTBs can be made by looking at their potentially measurable effects within the context of a static, deterministic, partial-equilibrium analysis of trade. Thus suppose, in figure 2.1, that import demand in the absence of an NTB can be modeled as perfectly competitive, and represented by the downward sloping demand curve, DD.[3] The import may be an imperfect substitute for a domestic good, in which case the position of DD depends on the price of the domestic substitute. Or it may be a perfect substitute for a domestic good, in which case DD is an excess demand curve. Although our comments here apply to both cases, some (but not all) of the formulas for measuring NTBs that we set forth in appendix 3 hold only for the case of perfect substitutes. Expressed in logarithms, let DD represent the quantity demanded, q, as a function of the domestic price paid by importers, p, in the absence of any NTB.[4]

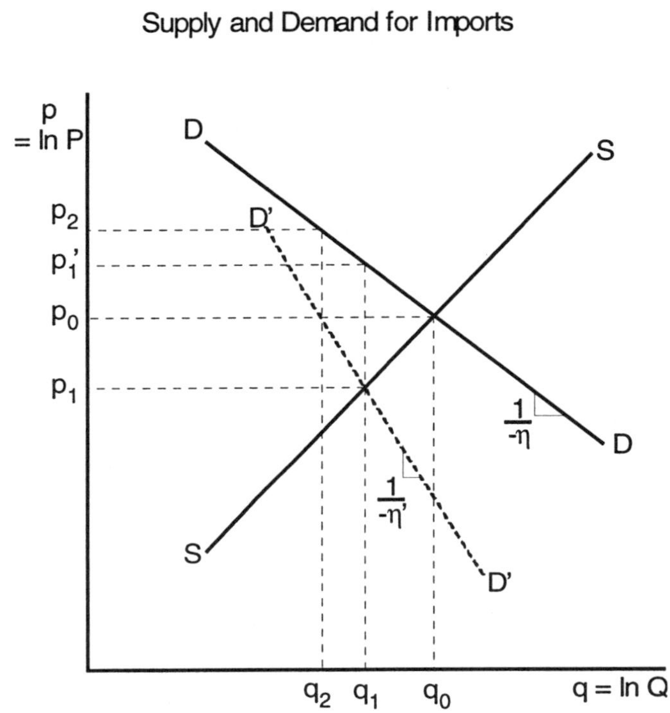

Figure 2.1
The Price and Quantity Effects of an NTB

Let the initial free-trade equilibrium price and quantity be p_0 and q_0, respectively, prior to the imposition of the NTB, assuming a competitive supply of exports from abroad as shown by the supply curve, SS. This is drawn as upward sloping, implying that the importing country is large enough to affect the world price of the good. A small country, in contrast, would face a horizontal supply curve. The formulas in appendix 3 are valid for both cases. Alternatively, foreign suppliers may have some degree of monopoly power, in which case no supply curve exists, and p_0 (and later p_1) is a profit-maximizing price or the outcome of an oligopolistic strategic interaction.

Now suppose that an NTB is introduced into this market. Without knowing the specific form that the NTB takes, we cannot know exactly how it will affect the market. However, interpreting the market price as that received by exporters, most NTBs can be thought of as shifting the import demand curve in some fashion.[5] For example, a direct quantitative restriction covering the entire industry will cause the import demand curve to become vertical at the permitted quantity, up to the price at which that quantity would be demanded voluntarily, and to coincide with the unconstrained demand curve for prices above that. Or, as another example, an industrial standard, the satisfaction of which adds a fixed (dollar) amount to the cost of each unit imported, can be thought of as shifting the demand curve downward and making it somewhat steeper.[6] These and other cases may be contrasted to what would be observed with a simple ad valorem tariff, that is, a parallel downward shift of the logarithmic demand curve. In all these cases the new demand curve indicates exporters' prices, which thus are net of the trade barrier. One must return to the original demand curve therefore to find the domestic price paid for the imported good, or its shadow price if the costs of the barrier are borne internally by the final user of the imported good.[7]

As these examples suggest, we can characterize trade barriers in general as changing both the shape and the position of the import demand curve, and we can describe the barriers in terms of what these changes are. Thus, let D′D′ be the new demand curve in the presence of the NTB. We have drawn it in figure 2.1 as both shifting to the left and becoming steeper (less elastic) because this is typical of many actual NTBs. But trade interference in general can change both the position and the slope of the demand curve in either direction.

Consider first changes in the position of the demand curve. These can be measured in either the price or quantity dimensions, and in addition—in either dimension—there are at least two frames of reference that can be used for capturing the shift of the curve. One of these frames of reference is more readily observable, while the other deals more precisely with the effects of the NTB itself.

In quantity terms, the easiest thing to observe in the figure is, of course, the actual decline in the quantity imported. This is the distance from q_0 to q_1 in figure 2.1 if the competitive supply curve SS is operative, or from q_0 to some other quantity if supply is not competitive.[8] In the price dimension, we may also be able to observe one or both of the prices, p_1 and p'_1, at which this new quantity is, respectively, supplied and demanded. For example, if the NTB is a quota that is allocated to domestic firms that resell on the domestic market, p_1 will be the price they pay for imports, p'_1 the price on the domestic market, and p'_1-p_1 the quota rent per unit, or quota premium. In other circumstances these prices may not be so easily observed. But if they can be observed, either the price difference, p'_1-p_1, or the change in domestic price, p'_1-p_0, can serve as handy measures of the size of the NTB.

The drawback of both these quantity and price measures, however, is that they reflect the interaction of supply and demand and not only the properties of the NTB itself. Thus, two NTBs in different markets that are in all formal respects identical could have quite different effects on actual prices and quantities in the two markets if supply conditions differ. Even if both are competitively supplied, the outcomes will depend on the supply elasticities, and even greater differences may occur if supplies are not competitive.

An alternative frame of reference that avoids this dependence on supply behavior requires that we normalize by comparing the two demand curves at, say, a constant price such as the free trade price.[9] Thus, holding price constant at p_0, we can measure the quantity effect of the NTB by the drop from q_0 to q_2—the amount that demand would be reduced by the NTB if the price paid to foreigners for the import were to remain unchanged. Corresponding to this quantity measure there is also an analogous price measure. The price p_2 represents the price that would induce buyers to reduce their purchases to q_2. The excess of p_2 over p_0, therefore, measures the NTB in a manner that can be directly compared to a tariff.[10]

These two approaches illustrate a basic difficulty that arises in the measurement of NTBs, even when one focuses on their most obvious price and quantity dimensions. In general, even if it is possible to observe what actually occurs as a result of the NTB, this does not in itself measure only the NTB, but captures other extraneous information, such as the supply elasticity, as well. The preferable measure of only the NTB itself requires information from what can usually be only a hypothetical experiment, such as implementing the NTB while holding the import price constant. Only in very special circumstances—specifically, if the supply of imports is both perfectly competitive and infinitely elastic—will the two measures be the same.

One other characteristic of an NTB that is obvious in figure 2.1 is the extent to which the elasticity of demand for imports is reduced. Since price and quantity are both expressed in logarithms in figure 2.1, the elasticity of demand is just (minus) one over the slope of the demand curve. As drawn, this elasticity (η') is smaller along D′D′ than (η) along DD, and this is typical of many NTBs. Certainly quotas, by restricting quantities of imports to a fixed amount independent of price, reduce the import demand elasticity substantially. While obviously this does not matter as long as we look only at a single static equilibrium, it can become very important when equilibria begin to change over time or in response to exogenous changes other than the NTB itself. We will have more to say about this in a moment.

Now it should be clear from even this simple example of NTBs in figure 2.1 that there is no single useful way of measuring the "size" of an NTB. Unlike tariffs, which are so well defined that a single number—the tariff rate—provides a complete description of the barrier in a given industry, NTBs require several parameters to characterize them fully.[11] At a minimum, just to draw figure 2.1, one needs to have either a price or a quantity measure of the shift in the demand curve, plus a measure of the amount by which the elasticity of demand is reduced. In addition, as we move beyond the simple framework of figure 2.1, there are still other characteristics of NTBs that should also be known if we are to anticipate fully their effects.

At this point, therefore, let us list all of the characteristics that we view as worth knowing in principle, whether or not there is any realistic hope of ever capturing them empirically. For completeness, we will begin by repeating those just mentioned, together with a brief explanation of why we view all of these characteristics as important.

1. *The Reduction in Quantity of Imports.* NTBs are most often imposed with the intent of reducing the quantity of imports. We have already noted at least two ways that this reduction could be defined, but, either way, such a measure is needed as the most direct indication of the trade restrictiveness of NTBs.

2. *The Increase in Price of Imports.* NTBs succeed in reducing the quantity of imports only to the extent that they raise the actual or shadow price of imports to demanders. This price increase has further implications for economic performance in other sectors of the economy, especially if the import is an intermediate input, and it is thus an important measure of the size of an NTB in its own right. In addition, the price effect of an NTB is more readily compared with a tariff than is the quantity reduction and, given the long experience with tariffs, therefore is more easily understood.[12]

3. *The Change in the Elasticity of Demand for Imports.* As already noted, NTBs often alter the slope of the demand curve for imports, and thus they alter the responsiveness of imports in a particular sector to price changes. Most often NTBs such as quotas reduce this elasticity, although it is also possible for some particular kinds of NTB to increase it. Either way, this can be a very important, though often neglected, measure of the importance of an NTB. Even if a quota does not significantly reduce imports at initial prices, for example, the constraint that it puts on changes in quantities may become important later if other conditions of supply or demand change for any reason. A reduced elasticity may also have a counterpart in the elasticity of demand facing competing domestic firms, and this is important for the competitive structure of the domestic industry. Finally, the elasticity effect of an NTB is also important in assessing, in a general equilibrium context, the role of NTBs in influencing the outcome of other events such as a change in tariffs. An increase in a tariff on a final good, for example, will have its protective effect reduced if there is an elasticity-reducing NTB in place on an important intermediate input.

4. *The Variability of NTBs.* Another important feature of NTBs is the extent to which their effects vary over time. Unlike tariffs, NTBs often are defined relative to a benchmark quantity or price that is set independently of market conditions. If this benchmark is held fixed when underlying conditions of supply and demand, exchange rates, and other market conditions change, as they inevitably do, then the effectiveness of the NTB will vary. Even if the benchmark is revised occasionally, it may over- or under-react to the market, and the revisions themselves may even increase the variability of the effects of the NTB. Such variability may constitute a neglected cost that the NTB imposes on society and thus is very important to measure along with its more obvious effects on average price and/or quantity.

5. *The Uncertainty of NTBs.* All government policies are uncertain in their implementation, but this seems to be especially true of some NTBs. Indeed, some practices such as antidumping and countervailing duty investigations have been identified as NTBs almost entirely because of the uncertainties that they impose on international traders. Even those barriers that are clearly restrictive, however, can become more so if their implementation is uncertain. This may be quite misleading, as, for example, in the case of a quota that may appear to be non-binding if potential traders fail to exhaust it because of uncertainty as to who among them is entitled to import. The importance of such uncertainty is clear to those who trade. Ideally, it should also be accounted for in attempts at measurement.

6. *The Welfare Costs of NTBs.* It is customary to measure the welfare costs of an NTB in the context of a diagram like figure 2.1 by using consumer and producer surplus to capture the welfare effects of distortions of consumer and producer behavior.[13] For this purpose the price and/or quantity measures of the NTB already discussed provide sufficient information. We mention these welfare costs separately because of their importance in the literature on NTBs.[14]

7. *Resource Costs of NTBs.* In addition to the traditional welfare costs just noted, there are also certain costs that are associated with the manner in which the NTB is administered.[15] First are the direct administrative costs themselves, that is, the resources used directly in enforcing whatever rules an NTB imposes.[16] Especially when the barriers themselves are not very restrictive, the presumption is that these costs, where they occur, are considerably larger than the traditional deadweight losses from distorted behavior. It is essential that more careful measurements of them be attempted. Second, and perhaps of much greater importance, are the resources lost to rent seeking and related phenomena. These are the time and other resources that are wasted by individuals and firms in their efforts to secure the profits and other benefits that are created by an NTB.

Conclusion

The preceding discussion has been designed to provide an overview of the variety of NTBs that may exist in different countries and to call attention to the characteristics of NTBs that will be important in trying to understand how to measure their size and their economic effects. Let us turn next accordingly to measurement issues. We first discuss general procedures for measuring NTBs, and we then take a more specific look at individual types of NTBs and the measurement issues that arise with each type.

CHAPTER 3

Methods of Measurement of Nontariff Barriers

In order to quantify the particular occurrence of an NTB, it is probably best to look at the specific details of the implementation of that NTB. For example, a quota usually permits an announced quantity of imports of a certain type, so that an analysis of the quota should begin with direct information pertaining to that quantity. Or to take another example, a variable levy is defined in terms of a specified price of an imported good, and that price provides the most direct information about what the levy entails. In these and other cases a good deal of additional work may be required, however, to translate this direct information into a useful form that can be understood and compared to other forms of trade intervention. Nonetheless this direct information still provides the most obvious starting point for an empirical analysis.

There are serious disadvantages to this direct approach, however, especially when one is looking for a broad measure of NTBs in general and not just of a specific type. First, the direct approach only captures those NTBs that have been identified. If a country or industry makes use of a particular form of NTB that the investigator does not take into account or include in the analysis, then trade may appear much freer than it actually is. Second, even for those NTBs that are included, it is extremely difficult to process the diverse direct information that is available on each NTB in a way that will be comparable across NTBs and thus permit them to be added up to obtain a total measure of trade interference. Third, if more than one NTB is present in a given industry, it is conceivable that the presence of one reduces the effects of another, so that an analysis of each of them separately may lead to an overstatement of their total effects. More generally, in evaluating overall levels of protection by NTBs, general equilibrium effects are bound to matter, such as the effects of barriers in one sector on trade in another, and the effects of all together on exchange rates. Thus even though direct information about NTBs is likely to be the most accurate available, it does not necessarily provide a good starting point for a general analysis.

Fortunately there exist a variety of more general approaches that can bypass some of these difficulties, though admittedly while introducing new ones. The various general methods that have been used or attempted for measuring NTBs can be classified as follows: *frequency-type measures* based upon inventory listings of observed NTBs that apply to particular countries, sectors, or categories of trade; *price-comparison measures* calculated in terms of tariff equivalents or price relatives; *quantity-impact measures* based upon econometric estimates of models of trade flows; and measures of *equivalent nominal rates of assistance*. We shall discuss each of these in turn. Thereafter, we consider some special purpose methods that may be useful in assessing some of the characteristics of NTBs that were identified in the preceding chapter. We shall then return to NTB-specific methods when we discuss several types of NTBs themselves. Finally, we discuss briefly issues arising in measurement of the *effects* of NTBs in which case measurement of the size of NTBs is a key input.

An issue that arises in common for all of these methods is how to aggregate the measurements once they have been obtained for disaggregated product categories. Most common, but also in many ways least satisfactory, is to use own-country imports as weights in calculating weighted averages of the NTBs in a larger product group. The obvious drawback is that the most restrictive NTBs reduce imports to zero, and therefore do not show up at all in the aggregate. Own-country production levels avoid this problem, but are subject to the opposite bias in that protective NTBs stimulate domestic production above the levels that would otherwise obtain. Preferable for many purposes, but also requiring data that may not be available, is to use world production levels or world trade as weights.

General Methods for Measuring the Presence or Size of NTBs

Frequency-Type Measures

In appendix 1, as already mentioned, we provide a list and brief description of the major types of existing NTBs and related policies. Since the detailed information collected especially by UNCTAD for its database on trade control measures is commodity/sector and country specific,[17] it is possible to construct a variety of measures that indicate the frequency of occurrence of NTBs.[18] Such measures may be unweighted, or they may be weighted by imports or by production. Examples are provided in tables 3.1 and 3.2 for the United States, the 12-member European Union (EU), Japan, and Canada for 1988 and 1993.[19]

Table 3.1 contains Frequency Ratios and Import Coverage Ratios for: "All" NTBs and "Hard core" NTBs;[20] Quantitative Restrictions (QRs), including export restraints, non-automatic licensing, and other QRs; and Price Control Measures (PCMs), including variable charges, antidumping/countervailing duties (AD/CVDs) and voluntary export price restraints (VEPRs), and other PCMs. The frequencies are calculated first for applicable Harmonized System (HS) commodity categories that were subject to some identifiable NTB in 1988 and 1993. The number of product categories subject to NTBs is then expressed as a percentage of the total number of product categories in each HS group. This is referred to as the Frequency Ratio (F). The

TABLE 3.1. Pervasiveness of Different Types of NTBs in OECD Countries in 1988 and 1993: the "Quad" (Percent)

NTB Categories	United States				EU-12				Japan				Canada			
	Frequency Ratio (F)		Import Coverage Ratio (IC)		Frequency Ratio (F)		Import Coverage Ratio (IC)		Frequency Ratio (F)		Import Coverage Ratio (IC)		Frequency Ratio (F)		Import Coverage Ratio (IC)	
	1988	1993	1988	1993	1988	1993	1988	1993	1988	1993	1988	1993	1988	1993	1988	1993
All NTBs	25.5	22.9	16.7	17.0	26.6	23.7	13.2	11.1	8.3	7.7	8.5	8.0	11.1	11.0	5.7	4.5
"Hard core" NTBs	25.5	22.9	16.6	17.0	25.2	21.8	10.9	9.0	7.6	7.0	7.2	3.6	8.9	8.2	4.1	2.5
Quantitative Restrictions (QRs)	20.4	18.1	13.7	10.2	19.5	17.2	7.8	7.1	7.3	6.7	6.5	2.8	6.6	6.8	3.0	1.7
Export Restraints	19.5	13.1	12.9	10.1	15.5	13.9	6.2	5.6	0.3	0.3	0.2	0.2	4.8	5.8	1.2	1.4
Non-automatic licensing	0.0	0.0	0.0	0.0	4.4	3.5	2.2	1.7	5.7	5.7	1.0	1.0	2.6	0.2	0.7	0.0
Other QRs	6.6	5.6	1.1	0.2	0.2	0.2	0.1	0.0	1.6	1.0	5.5	1.8	0.8	0.8	1.1	0.3
Price Control Measures (PCMs)	17.8	10.8	3.6	7.3	12.4	8.4	6.0	3.5	0.3	0.3	0.7	0.8	2.4	1.4	1.1	0.8
Variable charges	0.1	0.0	0.1	0.0	6.3	5.4	1.8	1.5	0.3	0.3	0.7	0.8	0.0	0.0	0.0	0.0
AD/CVs and VEPRs	17.8	10.8	3.4	7.3	2.6	1.9	2.2	1.3	0.0	0.0	0.0	0.0	2.4	1.4	1.1	0.8
Other PCMs	0.0	0.0	0.0	0.0	4.3	1.1	2.1	0.6	0.0	0.0	0.0	0.0	0.0	0.0	0.0	0.0

Note: "All NTBs" include: price control measures; finance measures; automatic licensing measures; quantity control measures; and monopolistic measures. "Core" NTBs, which are listed by sector in table 2, encompass "All NTBs" except for finance measures and monopolistic measures. "Hard core" NTBs include QRs and PCMs.

Source: OECD (1995, table 4.1).

Import Cover age Ratios (IC) in table 3.1 are calculated by determining the value of imports of each commodity subject to NTBs, aggregating by applicable HS commodity group, and expressing the value of imports covered as a percentage of total imports in theHS commodity group. The import weights are based on own-country imports for 1988 or an adjacent year. The 1988 import weights are used for the 1993 calculations. A sectoral breakdown for the "Core" NTBs is provided in table 3.2, which includes calculation of unweighted Frequency Ratios (F) and Production (i.e., gross output) weighted Frequency Ratios (PF).[21]

The results reported in table 3.1 suggest that the F and IC ratios for the EU-12, Japan, and Canada declined from 1988 to 1993. The F ratios for the United States declined, but some of the IC ratios increased. It is also evident that QR measures are more commonly used than PCMs in the "Quad" countries, and that there are differences among the countries in their reliance on particular types of NTBs. It appears in table 3.2 that "Core" NTBs are concentrated especially in: agricultural and food products; textiles and apparel; chemicals; nonmetallic mineral products; basic metals; and fabricated metals.[22]

The NTB measures in tables 3.1 and 3.2 are useful primarily in directing attention to the frequency of occurrence of various types of NTBs and the trade/production coverage of NTBs for individual countries and product groups for a given year and through time to the extent that the data are kept continuously. These measures have a number of drawbacks, however. First, according to OECD (1996), the reporting of NTBs is somewhat uneven, and there may be problems arising from how NTBs are defined and the level and type of aggregation used in calculating commodity and sectoral ratios. Second, the F and IC/PF ratios do not provide any information on the possible deterrent effects that NTBs may have upon the pricing or quantity decisions of foreign exporters. Third, the F and IC/PF ratios refer primarily to border measures and thus ignore the entire range of internal governmental measures and the restrictive actions of imperfectly competitive firms that we discussed earlier. Finally, and most importantly, the frequency-type measures provide no information on the economic impact that NTBs may have on prices, production, consumption, and international trade.[23] Worse, they may be positively misleading in this regard, if a large number of relatively small or non-binding NTBs divert attention from a smaller number in other industries or countries that have more serious effects.

Price-Comparison Measures

As indicated in figure 2.1, the effect of any NTB can be gauged in terms of its impact on the domestic price in comparison to some reference price. Because the price impact is a general property of NTBs, such a price comparison can pick up the net effects of all NTBs that are present in a market, without it be-

TABLE 3.2. Pervasiveness of "Core" NTBs in OECD Countries in 1988 and 1993: the "Quad" (Percent)

		United States				EU-12				Japan				Canada			
		Frequency Ratio (F)		Production-weighted Frequency Ratio (PF)		Frequency Ratio (F)		Production-weighted Frequency Ratio (PF)		Frequency Ratio (F)		Production-weighted Frequency Ratio (PF)		Frequency Ratio (F)		Production-weighted Frequency Ratio (PF)	
ISIC	Description	1988	1993	1988	1993	1988	1993	1988	1993	1988	1993	1988	1993	1988	1993	1988	1993
1	Agriculture, Forestry, Fishing	5.5	3.6	-	-	20.6	14.9	-	-	5.9	5.2	-	-	6.0	4.1	-	-
2	Mining and Quarrying	2.3	2.3	-	-	0.0	3.5	-	-	3.1	0.4	-	-	0.4	0.7	-	-
21	Coal Mining	0.0	0.0	-	-	0.0	0.0	-	-	-	-	-	-	8.3	0.0	-	-
22	Crude Petroleum	0.0	0.0	-	-	-	-	-	-	-	-	-	-	0.0	9.1	-	-
23	Metal Ore Mining	0.0	4.0	-	-	-	-			-	-	-	-	0.0	0.0	-	-
29	Other Mining	3.4	2.3	-	-	0.0	3.8	-	-	-	-	-	-	0.0	0.0	-	-
3	Manufacturing	27.3	24.7	17.2	17.9	26.2	22.8	7.7	6.0	7.9	7.4	2.1	1.8	9.4	8.8	8.2	6.8
31	Food, Beverages and Tobacco	14.5	12.1	18.4	15.8	50.7	44.2	0.0	0.0	11.2	6.7	10.8	7.9	14.2	11.4	26.2	22.8
32	Textiles and Apparel	82.6	69.9	84.1	71.8	73.8	76.8	66.5	79.5	21.3	21.4	20.1	20.1	35.2	41.5	40.2	41.6
33	Wood and Wood Products	3.5	0.6	3.9	0.7	0.0	0.0	0.0	0.0	0.0	0.0	0.0	0.0	1.8	3.2	2.4	4.3
34	Paper and Paper Products	1.3	1.3	1.5	1.5	2.7	0.4	1.2	2.6	0.0	0.0	0.0	0.0	1.1	1.2	1.5	1.7
35	Chemicals, Petroleum Products	8.7	5.8	8.6	7.0	5.4	5.1	2.4	5.7	0.8	0.7	1.0	0.8	1.5	0.3	1.8	0.4
36	Non-metallic Mineral Products	9.8	5.3	10.7	7.8	6.6	0.2	5.9	0.0	0.0	0.0	0.0	0.0	1.1	0.4	0.7	0.7
37	Basic Metal Industries	53.4	57.1	48.0	52.3	37.5	19.0	35.3	17.7	0.9	0.9	0.5	0.6	16.6	4.6	16.7	4.7
38	Fabricated Metal Products	10.2	13.8	14.8	20.1	4.1	2.3	4.4	1.8	0.0	0.0	0.0	0.0	1.4	1.4	0.8	0.6
39	Other Manufacturing	4.4	1.1	4.1	1.0	1.4	2.0	0.0	0.0	0.0	0.0	0.0	0.0	0.7	1.2	0.6	1.0
Total	**All Products**	**25.6**	**23.0**	**17.2**	**17.9**	**25.5**	**22.1**	**7.7**	**6.0**	**7.7**	**7.1**	**2.1**	**1.8**	**9.0**	**8.3**	**8.2**	**6.8**

Notes: "Core" NTBs exclude finance measures and monopolistic measures.
Source: OECD (1995, table 5.1).

ing necessary for the investigator to identify what those NTBs are. Thus price comparisons have provided the basis for much of the general empirical work that has tried to quantify them and not just identify where they occur.

We argued in connection with figure 2.1 that the purest measure of an NTB in the price dimension is one that compares p_0 with p_2. The first, p_0, is the price that would prevail without the NTB. The second, p_2, is the price that would prevail domestically in the presence of the NTB if the price paid to suppliers were to remain unchanged. However, because both of these prices are usually impossible to observe, actual measures of NTBs have focused instead on a comparison of the domestic and foreign prices in the presence of the NTB, p_1' and p_1. Letting *upper-case* letters represent the prices themselves, as opposed to their logarithms, these price comparisons are normally reported either as price relatives,

(1) $R = 100 \times P_1'/P_1$,

or as a percentage difference between the prices, comparable to a tariff,

(2) $T = 100 \times [P_1' - P_1]/P_1$.

In the latter form, depending on the particular prices used in the comparison, these measures are commonly referred to as *tariff equivalents, implicit tariffs, or implicit protective rates.*

1. Choosing Appropriate Prices. In order to apply this methodology it is necessary to identify the appropriate prices in data that are available. This is complicated largely because, at least at manageable levels of aggregation, goods of a particular "industry" that are imported into a country are seldom identical to other goods in that industry that are produced domestically. They may also differ from goods that are produced, sold, and perhaps traded elsewhere, abroad. Thus we may identify several different prices of the "good" in question, and these would not necessarily be equal to one another even if trade were perfectly free. It will be useful to give names to some of these prices[24]:

P_d^d—The price of the domestic substitutes for the imported good.

P_d^m—The price on the domestic market of the imported good itself.

P_d—The price of the good on the domestic market, independently of where it was produced; thus an index of P_d^d and P_d^m.

P_c^m—The (c.i.f.) invoice price of the imported good as paid by the domestic importer to the foreign exporter, inclusive of transport costs but excluding tariffs.

P_x^d—The invoice price received by an exporter of the good from the domestic country, exclusive of transport costs and export tax, if any.

In addition to all of these prices that relate to the domestic market, there is a comparable list for each other country of the world. These will be referred to in general with an asterisk (*) or with a country superscript.

Now we would argue that the appropriate prices to use in measuring an NTB are the domestic and invoice prices of the imported good, P_d^m and P_c^m. An example is given in table 3.3 for frozen chickens and frozen turkeys for Canada for 1980–85, taken from Moroz and Brown (1985, table D9). We recognize of course that it may be difficult to find adequate measures of P_d^m and P_c^m, depending on how general and aggregated is the analysis being conducted.[25] Thus domestic price measures typically do not distinguish domestically produced from imported goods. In this event, if P_d^m is not available, it may be necessary to use P_d instead. The "implicit tariff rate" may accordingly by calculated from the formula above for T but using P_d and P_i as the relevant prices:

(3) $IT^1 = 100 \times [P_d - P_c^m]/P_c^m$.

This is a valid measure of an NTB to the extent that the domestic and imported goods that are combined in P_d are perfect substitutes, so that they sell for the same price in the domestic market.[26] But in general, this measure has the serious disadvantage of incorporating information about the apparent substitutability of domestic and foreign goods. For example, a barrier that raises the domestic price of an import good by 10% may raise the price index in the domestic market by much less than that. This will happen if imports are only a small part of the market and if imports are also only a poor substitute for domestically produced goods in the same industry. Furthermore, if domestic varieties are of higher quality than imports, then this measure will find protection even if there is none. This method works best, then, for homogeneous products for which the invoice price of imports can either be observed directly, or constructed from the price on a unified world market.

In case the invoice prices of imports are also unavailable, an alternative is to make do with domestic prices only, but taken from a variety of countries:

(4) $IT^2 = 100 \times [P_d - P_d^*]/P_d^*$.

Here P_d^* may be either the domestic price in a particular foreign exporting country, in which case the measure may be of a bilateral NTB, or it may be the minimum domestic price among all foreign exporters. Thus, suppose that exporting firms are perfectly competitive or otherwise unable to price discriminate, and suppose also that all goods in the industry are perfect substitutes everywhere. Then domestic prices abroad will equal foreign export prices of the same goods, and this will be a valid method of measurement. However, this method will be even more subject to error from imperfect substitutability than the one described in the preceding paragraph, since both P_d and P_d^* will include prices of imperfect substitutes with which the traded good competes. In addition, if foreign suppliers can price discriminate between exports and their own domestic markets, P_d^* will overstate the prices of "dumped" imports and thus IT^2 will understate protection in the importing country. Finally, a basic difference between these two measures is that IT^2 includes transport costs while IT^1 does not.[27]

Examples of the first measure, in equation (3), are provided in table 3.4 for the United States for 1991 and 1993.[28] The results of the so-called price-gap measures for agricultural products may be considered reliable insofar as these products are reasonably homogeneous. The domestic prices used for motor vehicles and maritime transportation seem to us more problematic, however. Estimates of price-gap measures have also been made for several other OECD countries and will be discussed below.[29]

The second measure, in equation (4), can be illustrated in work by Campbell and Cossette (1994) noted in table 3.5. They compared Canadian domestic prices of such supply-managed products as dairy products and eviscerated chicken and turkey with constructed measures of reference prices for low-cost foreign suppliers, New Zealand and the United States. What is noteworthy about the results reported are the adjustments made to achieve comparability even for agricultural products that are ostensibly reasonably homogeneous.[30]

TABLE 3.3. Estimation of Tariff Equivalents for Poultry Products for Canada, 1980-1985

	1980	1981	1982	1983	1984	1985	Average
Estimation of Protection for Poultry Products[a]							
Price of Frozen Chickens[b]							
Canada[c]	70.4¢	91.0	88.8	94.7	103.9	92.4	90.2
U.S. (landed in Toronto)[d]	62.4	65.7	66.5	73.9	85.9	84.5	73.2
Estimate of Price Protection[e]	12.8%	38.5%	33.5%	28.2%	21.1%	9.4%	23.9%
Price of Frozen Turkeys[b]							
Canada[c]	91.7	111.0	115.4	110.3	118.6	132.7	113.3
U.S. (landed in Toronto)[d]	82.1	83.0	87.2	87.6	110.5	118.2	94.8
Estimate of Price Protection[e]	11.7%	33.7%	32.3%	25.9%	7.3%	12.3%	20.5%
Average Price Protection Provided to Poultry Product Producers[f]	12.3%	36.1%	32.9%	27.0%	14.2%	10.8%	22.2%

Notes:

[a]Tariff equivalent estimated by the price-comparison method.
[b]Price in cents per pound.
[c]Price in Toronto.
[d]Price in New York, in Canadian dollars, plus estimated transportation and processing costs.
[e]Estimated as difference between Canadian price and U.S. price, divided by U.S. price, measured in Canadian dollars and expressed in per cent.
[f]Average of estimates of price protection for chickens and turkeys.

Source: Adapted from Moroz and Brown (1985, table D9).

TABLE 3.4. Price-Gap Measures of U.S. Tariff Equivalents, by Sector, 1991 and 1993 (Percent)

Sector	1991	1993
Price-gap measures		
Agricultural sector[a]		
Sugar	124.8	93.7
Butter	26.9	20.8
Cheese	35.4	37.4
Dry/condensed mile products	60.3	60.3
Cream	60.3	60.3
Meat	6.5	5.0
Cotton	-	27.0
Motor vehicles[b]	-	0.4
Maritime transport (Jones Act)[c]	133.0	89.1

Notes:
[a]The price comparisons for the agricultural products were as follows. Sugar -- calculated as the difference between the U.S. price and the world price, inclusive of transport costs and import duties, expressed as a percentage of the world price; data from USDA, *Sugar and Sweetener: Situation and Outlook Yearbook*. Dairy products -- based on domestic and world price data collected by the USDA for whole milk powder, butter, and cheese; for dry/condensed milk products and cream, the price gap for whole milk powder was used as a proxy. Meat -- based on the "market price support" portion of the producer subsidy equivalent (PSE) calculated by the OECD, comparing Sioux Falls (U.S.) cutter prices with New Zealand milk cow prices, and weighted by imports from Australia and New Zealand. Cotton -- based on comparisons of U.S. domestic and world prices of Orleans/Texas "B" index cotton, including adjustments for transportation and marketing costs.
[b]Motor vehicles -- based on an estimated 1.5 percent additional increase above the industrywide U.S. price increase needed in Japanese autos to equate supply and demand in the presence of the auto import restraint; weighted by the percent of Japanese auto imports to total whole imports.
[c]Maritime transport -- calculated as the output-weighted average difference between the U.S. and world price for shipping "wet" and "dry" cargo; for wet cargo, the weighted differences are between the U.S. price for shipping Alaskan North Slope crude petroleum to the U.S. west coast and to the U.S. gulf coast and the average world price for comparable tanker shipments transported equal distances; a separate estimate from the literature was used for the tariff equivalent for dry cargo. Additional estimates of the price gap attributed to the Jones Act can be found in White (1988) and Francois et al. (1996, p. 186).

Sources: USITC (1993, 1995).

TABLE 3.5. Tariff Equivalents for Supply-Managed Products in Canada, 1979-1992

	1979	1988	1992
Dairy			
Cdn. Unit Value of Delivered Milk (C$/T)[a]	258.5	417.2	460.0
Reference Price (C$/T)[b]	136.3	187.2	174.4
Price Difference (C$/T)	122.2	230.2	285.6
Price Difference (%)	89.7	123.0	164.8

Chicken			
Cdn. Price Eviscerated (C$/T)[c]	1,190.1	1,526.6	1,560.6
Reference Price (C$/T)[d]	1,004.5	1,286.6	1,221.8
Price Difference (C$/T)	185.6	258.0	338.7
Price Difference (%)	18.5	20.1	27.7
Turkey			
Cdn. Price Eviscerated (C$/T)[e]	1,490.8	1,817.8	1,732.1
Reference Price (C$/T)[f]	1,387.8	1,376.7	1,341.6
Price Difference (C$/T)	103.1	441.1	390.8
Price Difference (%)	7.4	32.0	29.1

[a]Includes fluid milk, industrial milk and cream.
[b]Based on New Zealand price, adjusted to reflect fat content, currency exchange and transportation charges to Canada.
[c]Based on average price for broiler chicken under 2.3 kgs. Data refer to Toronto live price to producer -- 1979 and 1988: *Poultry Market Review*, annual, table 6 - 1992; *Agri-food Perspectives*, July 1992, Agriculture Canada, table 12. Prices converted to an eviscerated basis.
[d]Based on average U.S. live price for 1979. For 1988 and 1992: USDA publication: "Situation and Outlook Report of Livestock and Poultry," May 1992, table 2. Prices adjusted to an eviscerated basis, and to reflect transportation charges to Canada and currency exchange.
[e]Based on average price for broiler turkey under 5.4 kgs. Data refer to Toronto live price to producer -- 1979 and 1988: *Poultry Market Review*, Annual, table 7 -- 1992: *Agri-food Perspectives,* July 1992, Agriculture Canada, table 12. Prices converted to eviscerated basis.
[f]Based on average U.S. live price for 1979. For 1988 and 1992: USDA publication: "Situation Outlook Report of Livestock and Poultry," May 1992, table 13. Prices adjusted to an eviscerated basis, and to reflect transportation charges to Canada and currency exchange.

Source: Adapted from Campbell and Cossette (1994, table 7).

2. Quota-Auction and Quota-Transfer Price Measures. In addition to the foregoing, we should also mention quota-auction and quota-transfer price measures, the latter of which have been calculated in connection with the Multifiber Arrangement (MFA). If rights to import or export under a quota are sold at auction, then the auction price becomes an obvious measure of the quota's restrictiveness. More commonly, as in the MFA, quotas are allocated directly to firms, but the firms are then allowed to transfer these quotas to other firms, and a market develops for their exchange. The market price of these quota-transfers conveys similar information to an auction price, and we will use the term "auction price" to encompass both.

The MFA can be characterized as a voluntary export restraint (VER) in which the import quotas are allocated to foreign suppliers. We have assumed thus far with respect to import quotas that the import licenses are allocated to competitive firms in the importing country, in which case measurement of the price effects of the NTB can be analyzed as already indicated. Alternatively, if the licenses are allocated to foreign suppliers, the import price becomes effectively the domestic price in the importing country, assuming that the foreign supplier captures all the rents involved. To measure the size of the NTB associated with the VER, we therefore need information on the price of the good in the exporting country $\left(P_d^*\right)$ and the auction price of the quota (A). The tariff equivalent of the VER is given by:

$$(5) \qquad IT^{3}_{VER} = 100 \times A/P_d^*$$

In interpreting equation (5), it should be noted that if the VER is not binding, the auction price of the quota should be zero. If the auction price is not zero, then the ostensibly non-binding quota is still having an effect.[31] Furthermore, if market conditions are imperfectly competitive, some of the rents may be captured by importers. The availability of appropriate data also poses serious problems of measurement, although as the name suggests, if the licenses are allocated by a formal and public auction, the auction prices may be public knowledge, making this one of the easiest NTBs to measure. More commonly, however, VERs are allocated directly to firms and measurement of A is problematic, requiring knowledge of the prices charged by these firms in both their domestic and foreign markets.

In some cases as noted, while no auction may be used to allocate the quota initially, a secondary market for the transfer of quota rights may be permitted. The market prices of these transfers may then be used in place of A. One should take care, however, to obtain a representative sample of transfer prices, since they may vary over time and space.

Table 3.6 gives examples of quota-transfer price measures for several types of U.S. imports of textile and apparel products under the MFA for 1991 and 1993. These measures rely heavily on estimates of Hong Kong export prices and quota-transfer prices. Application to other supplying countries is based on adjusting the Hong Kong data to take into account relative differences in labor costs and gross output per worker in the individual MFA product categories.[32]

TABLE 3.6. Quota-Auction Price Measures of U.S. Tariff Equivalents of Textiles and Apparel by Sector, 1991 and 1993 (Percent)

Sector	1991	1993
Quota-auction price measures		
Textiles:		
Broadwoven fabric mills	8.5	9.5
Narrow fabric mills	3.4	3.3
Yarn mills and textile finishing	5.1	3.1
Thread mills	4.6	2.2
Floor coverings	2.8	9.3
Felt and textile goods, n. e. c.	1.0	0.1
Lace and knit fabric goods	3.8	5.9
Coated fabrics, not rubberized	2.0	1.0
Tire cord and fabric	2.3	2.4
Cordage and twine	3.1	1.2
Nonwoven fabric	0.1	0.2
Apparel and fabricated textile products:		
Women's hosiery, except socks	5.4	2.3
Hosiery, n. e. c.	3.5	2.4
Apparel made from purchased materi-	16.8	19.9

als		
Curtains and draperies	5.9	12.1
House furnishings, n. e. c.	8.3	13.9
Textile bags	5.9	9.0
Canvas and related products	6.3	5.2
Pleating, stitching, trimmings, and schiffli embroidery	5.2	7.6
Fabricated textile products, n. e. c.	9.2	0.6
Luggage	2.6	10.4
Women's handbags and purses	1.0	3.1

Notes: Tariff equivalents for U.S. imports from Hong Kong were estimated on the basis of average weekly Hong Kong quota prices paid by brokers, using information from International Business and Economic Research Corporation. For countries that do not allocate quota rights in public auctions, export prices were estimated from Hong Kong export prices, with adjustments for differences in labor costs and productivity. It was assumed that

$P_e^o = (W_o/W_{hk})\ (go_{hk}/go_o)P_e^{hk}$, where P_e^o $P_e^o = (W_o/W_{hk})(go_{hk}/go_o)P_e^{hk}$, where P_e^o is the export price of the other exporter country, W_o and W_{hk} are labor costs for apparel in other exporting countries and Hong Kong, go_o and go_{hk} are gross output per worker, and P_e^{hk} is the Hong Kong export price. Assuming that exports from all countries are subject to the same transportation costs and are perfect substitutes, the implied auction price from the other country, A^o, can then be inferred from that for Hong Kong, A^{hk}: $A^o = A^{hk} + P_e^{hk} - P_e^o$, or zero if this expression is negative. Trade weights were used for purposes of aggregation. See USITC (1995, pp. 3-5) for sources of data on labor costs and productivity.

Sources: USITC (1993, 1995).

There have been numerous estimates of the MFA quota tariff equivalents for other OECD countries, some of which will be noted in chapter 4. They are of course subject to the caveats already mentioned. We shall also discuss further aspects of VERs in our treatment of NTB-specific methods of measurement.

3. Measures of Equivalent Nominal Rates of Assistance. While our discussion thus far has focused mainly on border policies that restrict trade, those who have used these measurements for the purpose of estimating assistance to industry have had to take into account other domestic policies. A more comprehensive measure is therefore needed that can aggregate all of the different types of incentives or disincentives that may exist. Two such measures that may be calculated are: (1) the nominal rate of assistance on outputs (NRA); and (2) the nominal rate of assistance on materials (NRM) (intermediate inputs). The NRA of an industry reflects those policies, such as tariffs and other border measures, that raise the price of the industry's output. The NRM of an industry, in contrast, reflects those policies that raise the prices of inputs to the industry, thus taking account of policies in other industries and the input-output interactions among industries. An indication of the component policies included in the NRA and NRM measures by the Industry Commission of the Commonwealth of Australia and definitions of these measures are provided in appendix 2. The NRA and NRM, in turn, provide the basis for calculating the effective rate of assistance (ERA), which is analogous to the effective rate of protection (ERP) and is a measure of the structure of net incentives affecting particular sectors. Under certain specified assumptions, which we shall discuss in more detail below, measures of the ERA can be used to analyze how the structure of net incentives may affect the allocation of labor and capital among the sectors of an economy.

4. Conclusion. Price-comparison measures of tariff equivalents have an intuitive appeal, especially since they give the appearance of having the same properties as nominal tariff rates themselves. This is misleading, however, since, as our discussion suggests, there are some potentially serious conceptual as well as data problems that arise in the estimation and interpretation of tariff equivalents.

Quantity-Impact Measures

We noted in reference to figure 2.1 above that the shift of the import demand curve due to an NTB can be defined in either the price or the quantity dimension. This suggests that the measurement of this shift could also be accomplished by looking at quantities of imports, as an alternative to looking at prices. Indeed Jager and Lanjouw (1977) have argued that a quantity measure is preferable to a price measure in that it comes closer to telling us what we really want to know about the *effects* of an NTB: that is, *by how much it reduces trade*. They argue further that price measures such as tariff equivalents fail to provide this information, since the relationship between the price and quantity effects of an NTB is a complicated one involving all of the elasticities of demand, domestic supply, and foreign supply.[33] Thus a direct measure of the quantity reduction due to an NTB would be desirable, if only as a supplement to the information provided by prices.

Unfortunately, there does not seem to be any way of getting such a direct measure of the quantity effects of an NTB that would be analogous to the price impact measures just discussed. While the quantity that is imported under the NTB is observable, there is usually no other quantity against which to compare it. For particular NTBs, if it is known when they are and are not in effect, it may be possible to build a time-series econometric model of the imports that they cover and thus to estimate what imports would have been without the NTB. But this is an NTB-specific method, and we will discuss it below.[34]

A general approach to measurement of the quantity effects of NTBs is possible, however, using either a cross-commodity or a cross-country regression model to explain trade. Thus the object again is to estimate what trade would have been in the absence of NTBs and to compare this to the trade that actually does occur. To do so requires a satisfactory model of the determinants of trade, as well as data covering a sufficient variety of trading situations. The latter are needed in order to identify, or extrapolate to, a situation in which trade is at least approximately free.

The work that is relevant here stems from the substantial literature on the gravity model that has been developed over the years to investigate the interrelated questions of what determines the size of a nation's foreign sector and/or the flow of trade among or between countries. As Leamer and Stern (1970, pp.

151–52) note, the important determinants involve a nation's GNP, resource endowment, utility structure, and various resistance factors.[35] In the broadest sense, this research can be interpreted as an effort to understand the forces that shape comparative advantage and at the same time to account explicitly or implicitly for a variety of special factors that may diminish or augment a nation's trade.[36] Thus, what we are interested in are the effects of NTBs on trade.

There are several different approaches that have been used to provide the basis for econometric estimates of NTBs. These approaches can be characterized as being based on stylized or formal versions of the Heckscher–Ohlin, Helpman–Krugman, and gravity models of international trade. Essentially, all of these approaches attempt to measure NTBs, either by regarding residuals from the estimated regressions as representing NTBs or by using various dummy variables. That is, the intention is to reflect departures from comparative advantage and thus to identify industries and countries in which trade intervention may possibly diminish or augment trade performance. While it is useful to have such general evidence of the trade impact of policy interventions by industry and country, these approaches share some important drawbacks.[37]

First, by attributing to NTBs all departures of trade from what the included variables can explain, there is a tremendous burden on the model that is used to explain trade. Indeed, the worse is the model of trade flows, the greater—most likely—will be the estimates of NTBs, suggesting a considerable upward bias in their estimation.[38] Second, it can be argued that theoretical trade models are capable of determining patterns of trade only when a series of highly unrealistic assumptions are made. In their absence, such models can only determine patterns of trade in an average sense, and they are not adequate to the task of predicting trade exactly for particular industries and countries. Thus a departure of actual trade from what is predicted by a regression model may reflect only this indeterminacy and not the presence of NTBs. Third, these approaches can really only make comparisons among industries or countries. They cannot tell us how far trading patterns depart from free trade. For if NTBs restrict trade everywhere, that may be imbedded in the parameters of the regressions and will not be reflected in the residuals or coefficients of the dummy variables used to represent unusual circumstances. For these reasons, one should be very cautious in using the results based on estimates of trade models. At best, such estimates may be most helpful for identifying relative levels of nontariff protection across sectors and countries.[39]

Special Purpose Methods

Having reviewed a number of general procedures for measuring NTBs, it may be worth considering some alternative measures that may be promising and that could shed light on some of the particular issues raised in chapter 2 concerning the characteristics of NTBs. These alternative measures include: (1)

elasticity estimation; (2) determinants of variations in elasticity estimates; (3) variations in effects of NTBs over time; (4) binding of NTBs; and (5) risk characteristics of NTBs.[40]

1. Elasticity Estimation. We noted in discussing figure 2.1 that many NTBs are likely to reduce the elasticity of import demand. This suggests that it might be worthwhile to perform a time series estimation of import demand elasticities, in the aggregate or for individual commodities/sectors, using data from several countries and interactive country dummy variables in order to determine how these elasticities may differ across countries. This should provide an indication of the extent to which the price responsiveness of import demand is reduced by NTBs in some countries more than others. Such a measure could be quite general in its coverage, since it would include even cultural barriers and other institutional factors that may restrict trade.

2. Variations in Elasticity Estimates. There is a vast empirical literature in which import demand elasticities have been estimated. Most of the important efforts were surveyed some time ago in Stern, Francis, and Schumacher (1976) and in Goldstein and Khan (1984), but there have not been any more recent surveys. It would nonetheless be worthwhile to review the recent literature to compile the elasticity estimates that may exist for a variety of countries and industries and to use regression methods to explain the variations in these estimates in terms of country and industry characteristics.[41] The regression residuals would then provide another estimate of how the price responsiveness departs from what it would otherwise be, presumably again because of the general existence of NTBs.

3. Effects of NTBs over Time. Our discussion in connection with figure 2.1 was based upon given underlying demand and supply conditions. If these conditions change for any reason, and assuming the NTBs themselves remain intact, then the effects of the NTBs will be altered. In order to determine how these effects vary over time, it might be worth repeating any one or more of the methods noted above for a succession of years. This would apply as well if the NTBs themselves were to change over time.

4. Binding of NTBs. It would be desirable to know to what extent various restrictions are binding, and how this varies over time. This could be done by calculating either the permitted or potential level of imports and then comparing this with actual imports. The comparisons will be significant insofar as the effects of NTBs will surely depend on whether the NTBs are fully or partially binding or not binding at all.[42]

5. Risk characteristics of NTBs. It is widely acknowledged that in the past decade or more there has been an increase in the use of contingent or administered protection, in particular antidumping and countervailing duty actions. Trading firms may thus be confronted with uncertainty over whether they will be subject to NTBs and, if they are, what the size and impact may be. It would be worthwhile accordingly to determine if there are any indicators of the costs that firms face when there is uncertainty regarding the imposition of NTBs. For example, trading firms may adapt their behavior in light of the risks involved, and the question is how they do this and what the costs to them are.[43]

NTB-Specific Methods for Selected NTBs

We turn now to consider measurement problems for some of the most important types of NTBs. Our main objective is to determine the extent to which these NTBs will be adequately captured by the various methods of measurement discussed above. In addition, where possible, we will discuss NTB-specific methods of measurement that may be appropriate to these particular NTBs. To both of these ends, we will begin each case with a brief discussion of how each kind of NTB works, together with a simple theoretical analysis of it.

Before proceeding, we should mention one method of empirical analysis that is applicable to any kind of NTB, but that works only if you know what the NTB is. In many instances, particular NTBs are implemented at a given point in time. With that information alone it may be possible to identify the effects of the NTB just by observing how the price or quantity of imports change at the time of implementation. Or, more elaborately if data are available, one can do a time-series econometric analysis for the periods in which the NTB is in place.[44] Either way, this provides a very straightforward way of analyzing a known barrier to trade.

The method is not without its shortcomings, however. Unless the implementation of the NTB comes as a complete surprise to the public, it is likely to have effects—perhaps perverse ones—long before it is put formally in place. These effects may thus detract from the usefulness of this method of measurement. Also, as always with econometric analysis, the results are only as valid as the model that is used to fit the data. If some other event happens to affect trade simultaneously with the NTB, then this approach may give misleading information unless the importance of that other event is correctly diagnosed.

Quotas

Quotas are the most straightforward of NTBs, and while they are often thought of as the most obvious and typical NTB, their relative simplicity is misleading since it is not shared by other forms of NTB. An import quota is simply a quantitative restriction on imports.[45] That is, a country desiring to restrict imports of a particular good determines the amount that it wishes to let in during a given year, say, and then prohibits any quantity beyond that from entering its borders. We shall assume that those units of the good that do come in do so without a tariff.[46] However, the forced scarcity of imports inevitably raises the price of the good on the domestic market by the amount necessary to sufficiently reduce demand. This in turn means that, somewhere along the chain of transactions that gets the good from the foreign to the domestic market, a premium is added to its price.

This can be illustrated along the same lines as in figure 2.1. Let DD′ in figure 3.1 be the logarithmic demand curve in the absence of any quota. Now impose a quota on the entire industry, prohibiting imports from exceeding the quantity $\hat{q}$. From the point of view of the world market, it appears as though the demand curve has changed to the broken curve DABC, with a kink at A, because at any price below $\hat{p}$ only the demand for $\hat{q}$ will be felt on the world market. Given the supply curve SS′, for imports from the world market, the world price will fall to p_l. However, since demand for the imported good domestically is unchanged, its price on the domestic market must rise to $\hat{p}$, in order to reduce demand to the required level. Since demanders of the good pay $\hat{p}$, only p_l of which reaches the foreign suppliers, the difference $\hat{p}-p_l$ is the premium that must be received by somebody. As we have already mentioned, the exact nature of this premium, and who gets it, both depend on how the quota is administered.

The method of administration that most economists would prefer, but which governments only occasionally use, involves the auctioning of import licenses. That is, at the beginning of each year, say, the government would print up licenses to import the quantity set by the quota for that year, and it then would auction them off in open competitive bidding. Allowing these licenses also to be resold on a secondary market thereafter, competition will establish the price of one of these licenses equal to the anticipated difference between the price of the good on the domestic market and its price on the world market—or $\hat{p}-p_l$, in figure 3.1.[47] As the year goes by, the supply and demand curves are likely to shift and this price will fluctuate. Aside from that fluctuation, however, this method of administering the quota comes close to replicating a tariff equal to the price of the license, since it not only raises the domestic price above the world price, but also allows the government to acquire the price difference as revenue.

A second way of administering a quota is to allocate the rights to import fixed amounts free of charge among importing firms. Once the allocation is made, the firms receive the price difference between the domestic and world markets as a pure rent. If the allocation is made among a sufficiently large number of firms, then they will still compete among themselves on the domestic market and will end up charging a single competitive price. But that price will be $\hat{p}$, enough above the world price to clear the domestic market. The situation is again analogous to a tariff, although here the "revenues" from

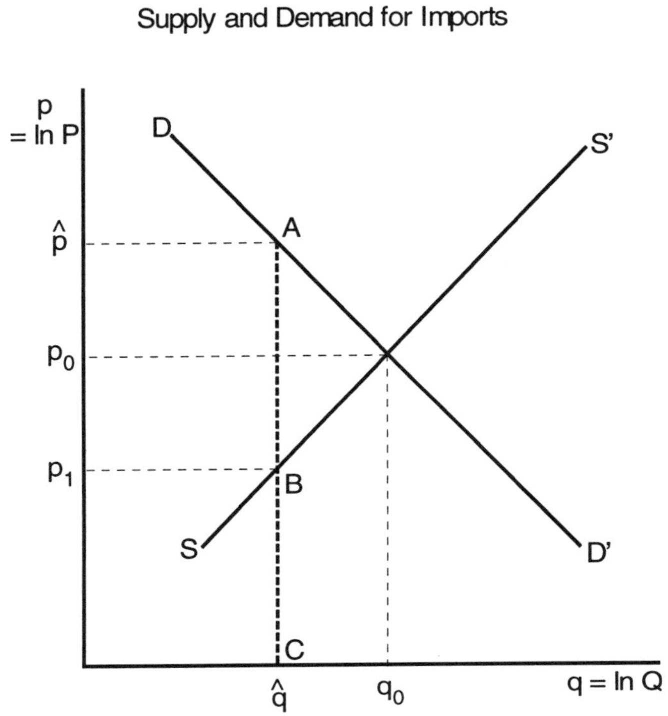

Figure 3.1
The Price and Quantity Effects of a
Quota or a Variable Levy

the NTB, or quota rents, accrue to the firms who were allocated the rights to import.

Additional distortions are possible, however, depending on how the allocation is made among firms. If the allocation is made on a political basis, for example, then potential importing firms will have an incentive to bid for licenses in the political market, by lobbying or whatever other mechanism is acceptable in the country. If the allocation is made on economic grounds, then there is an incentive for firms to distort the behavior that is to be used as an economic indicator. For example, if allocations are to be based on firm size as measured by the book value of capital stocks, then the quota rents become part of their return to capital, and firms have an incentive to over-invest. Or if allocations are on the basis of domestic sales, and if firms have access to a domestic source of supply, then they will expand their domestic supplies beyond even what would be indicated by the elevated domestic price in order to capture more of the quota rents. Clearly there is no end to the list of distortions that could be created by alternative mechanisms of allocating the quota.[48]

There are other ways that a quota could be administered, some of them causing much greater variations in the behavior of the market.[49] The point is merely that the method of administering a quota can make a great deal of difference as to its effects. This underscores the importance that we noted above in chapter 2 of getting as full a characterization as possible of any NTB, since even the seemingly simple quota can be quite complex.

With this sketch of the effects of a quota as background, consider now what difficulties quotas may pose for the methods of general empirical analysis discussed above. That is, can we expect those methods such as the ones reported in tables 3.1–3.6 to do an adequate job of capturing any quotas that are present among the array of NTBs?

Regarding the frequency-type measures, the answer seems to be yes, although of course these measures do not tell us very much. For their purpose, however, quotas have the advantage of being quite visible and easily understood. Because of the formal administrative procedures that they require, it should not be difficult to document the existence of quotas where they occur, as we have already illustrated in tables 3.1 and 3.2.

Regarding the price-comparison measures, however, there are at least three reasons why quotas may pose difficulty in addition to the problems of imperfect substitution with domestic goods discussed above for particular prices used to measure NTBs. Two of these reasons cause price comparisons to understate the severity of a quota, or even miss it entirely, while the third works in the opposite direction.

First, the price $\hat{p}$ in figure 3.1 is the equilibrium price facing domestic demanders of the good, but it is a market price only if these demanders are other than the importers who receive the quota allocations. Not infrequently, though, when quotas are applied to imports of intermediate goods, they are allocated directly to the using firms who are also discouraged from reselling them. In that case, $\hat{p}$ is still a relevant price for measuring the quota, but it is a shadow price and not observable.[50]

Second, other difficulties may arise on the supply side. If foreign supply is really perfectly competitive, and if in addition foreign governments do not change policies in response to the quota, then there is no problem. But if either foreign firms or foreign governments have the power to raise the price at which the good is supplied (the latter perhaps through an export tax), it is clearly in their interest to do so. If that happens, then the invoice price for imports may be not much below $\hat{p}$, even though the quota is no less restrictive. Together, these first two phenomena could completely invalidate at least one of the price-impact measures discussed above in equations (3) and (4).[51]

The third phenomenon works in the opposite direction. This is the well-known tendency for exporters under a quota to upgrade their product lines, exporting higher quality products than before the quota. This enables them to maximize the return on their import licenses and causes their prices to consumers to rise even more than if such upgrading did not take place. In an industry study of a particular NTB this can be taken account of by hedonic pricing methods,[52] but this is impossible in a general study of NTBs across industries. Thus for various reasons price-comparison measures may provide an inexact picture of the tariff equivalent and general incidence of quotas.

The trade-flow regression measures mentioned above fare better with a quota, since these measures tend to focus on quantities rather than prices. Except where smuggling is a serious problem, quantities traded should be more easily measured than prices. The only difficulty we see is that quotas, if they are not always binding, seem to impose such markedly nonlinear behavior that it may be difficult to specify appropriate functional forms for regression models.

Consider finally what specific method would be best if one only wished to measure a particular quota. The quantity to be admitted under the quota is usually readily available information, but by itself it is not very informative. About all it can indicate easily is—by comparing it with actual imports under the quota—whether the quota is binding or not. This is important information, as we noted earlier, but it is not very much.

Other more useful information about a quota may be available depending on the method of administration. Where import licenses are used to allocate the quota, the price of these licenses on the open market—whether purchased from the government or from other firms—can be an excellent source of information on the price impact of the quota. In fact, as already mentioned in connection with the MFA measurements, such information has been used for this purpose.[53]

If quota licenses are not auctioned or marketed, then some sort of price comparison is likely to be the next best alternative. Which particular price comparison is feasible and appropriate depends on the substitutability of the imported good with domestic alternatives, as well as the availability of various price data. Several methods are laid out in appendix 3, and a guide to their use is provided in our concluding chapter 5. The methods include:

(1) comparison of domestic prices with the c.i.f. prices of imports;
(2) comparison of import prices with prices of comparable exports to other countries; and
(3) comparison of domestic prices in the importing and exporting countries.

Whatever may be the most appropriate feasible price comparison, the value of any of these measures will depend on the care that has been taken to collect the needed price data.

If license prices are not available or are not useful because of supply-side responses to the quota, and if price comparisons are infeasible due to lack of data, then there is probably no alternative but to build a careful econometric model of the trade in question and use it to determine, for comparison, what trade would have been without the quota. This of course corresponds to the more general method alluded to above.

Variable Levies

Variable levies are much more specialized than quotas, having been used historically to protect agriculture in the European Community and in Sweden.[54] But we consider them next because they can be thought of as the mirror image of quotas. That is, while a quota fixes the quantity of imports, a variable levy fixes their price. This is done by the mechanism of charging what is essentially a tariff, the size of which varies, however, to achieve the desired domestic price of the import. The variation in the levy is instantaneous, it being left up to the customs officers at the border to charge an amount equal to the difference between the target price and the invoice price.[55]

Formally, figure 3.1 still applies. If the target price of the levy is $\hat{p}$, then again it is as though the world faces a demand for imports that is distorted to the curve DABC. The reason is that a fall in the world price below $\hat{p}$ will just cause the levy to be raised, keeping domestic price at $\hat{p}$ and thus keeping quantity demanded at $\hat{q}$.

This formal equivalence in static terms is misleading, however. There are important differences between the two NTBs if one considers changes in underlying conditions within the importing country.[56] If the demand curve for imports were to shift to the right, for example, a quota would hold quantity constant while forcing the domestic price to rise, whereas a variable levy would hold the domestic price constant and permit the full increase in demand to be imported. Correspondingly, the tariff equivalent of the quota, if it can be measured, will rise due to such an increase in demand, while the tariff equivalent of the variable levy will fall.

If a variable levy could be implemented as easily as just described, the analogue of the rents from a quota would simply go to the importing-country government as revenue from the levy. In fact, however, there is an incentive problem with this scheme that may interfere with the government collecting these revenues in full. Given that the levy will vary to achieve the target domestic price and that the importer knows this, it is a matter of indifference to him what price he pays, up to $\hat{p}$, for the imported good. The foreign exporter therefore faces little constraint in raising his price, even in competition with other exporters, since the importer has no incentive to buy from the cheapest supplier. Presumably the importing-country government can try to prevent such overcharging by monitoring world prices, but this is bound to be difficult. Therefore we expect the invoice price in a market with a variable levy to lie somewhere above p_1.

Empirically, then, the effects of a variable levy may be deceptively difficult to measure. Exactly as in the case of a quota, where foreign suppliers may respond by raising price, the difference between the domestic and invoice prices, if it were known, would not provide an accurate gauge of the size of the barrier that the variable levy entails. For the same reason the size of the levy itself would not be as informative as one would expect.[57] Instead one must get at the effects of a levy more indirectly, perhaps by comparing domestic and world prices as in the formula for IT^2 in equation (4) above. Two such measures are provided in appendix 3.

Voluntary Export Restraints

A form of protection that has been of great importance, especially in the two decades prior to conclusion of the Uruguay Round in 1995, both in the United States and elsewhere, is the Voluntary Export Restraint (VER). Also called a Voluntary Restraint Agreement and similar to an Orderly Marketing Arrangement,[58] a VER is an action undertaken by an exporting-country government to restrict exports of a particular good to a particular importing country, done at the instigation of the importing-country government. Since the restriction is stated in terms of the quantity of exports, it is identical to an export quota except for its political motivation.

A simple model of an export restraint is shown in figure 3.2 under the assumption that there is only a single foreign exporting country supplying the imported good.[59] The free-trade supply and demand curves for imports into the domestic country are SS′ and DD′ as before, with free-trade equilibrium price and quantity, p_0 and q_0. The VER restricts exports to the quantity $\hat{q}$, and results in a new kinked supply curve SBAC, since foreign exporters will be restrained from supplying more than $\hat{q}$ even at prices higher than p_1. To achieve this reduction on the part of competitive suppliers, either the actual or the shadow price they receive for exports of the good must fall to p_1. This could be accomplished, for example, by auctioning off export licenses, the price of which would then be $\hat{p} - p_1$.

Because a VER is really just an export quota, much of what we said above about quotas applies here as well. In particular, if domestic import firms have any monopsony market power, they will reduce the price paid to foreign exporters below $\hat{p}$, taking part of the quota rents for themselves. Likewise, the shadow price of exports to the foreign firms, p_1, will be difficult to observe since the export licenses will likely be allocated directly to producers, rather than to independent foreign traders who would buy the good on the open market. Thus direct price comparisons will be difficult as a means of measuring the effects of a VER,[60] and a general approach to measuring NTBs by comparing price indices may understate the effects of VERs. Nonetheless, if exporters who are subject to the VER sell in another market as well, either another export market or their own domestic market, then a comparison of prices in these markets may make it possible to circumvent these difficulties. In appendix 3 we provide several such formulas that may be applied, depending on the circumstances.

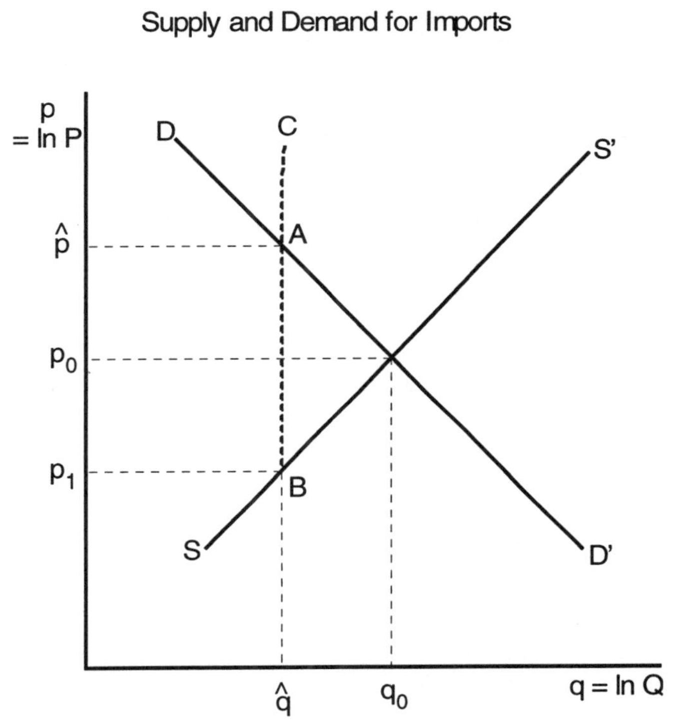

Figure 3.2
The Price and Quantity Effects of a
Voluntary Export Restraint

In some cases of VERs, quantity effects may be easier to get at than prices, since the quantities permitted by the VER and the quantity actually traded are both observable. However to compare either of these to the quantity that would have been traded without the VER requires accurate modeling of the industry's supply and demand behavior over time.[61,62]

Government Procurement Regulations

There are many ways in which demanders in a country may show a nationalistic preference for their own products over imports, either from the world generally or from particular foreign countries. A notable example of such preference is government procurement regulations, which typically may require purchasers for government agencies to show a preference for domestically produced goods. For example, there may be an explicit or tacit requirement that imports be avoided unless they fall below the price of domestic goods by more than a certain stated percentage. This is the kind of NTB that was the subject of one of the codes negotiated in the Tokyo Round and further expanded in coverage in the Uruguay Round. Some governments have as a consequence agreed not to engage in this kind of behavior in a number of areas that were negotiated. Nonetheless, it is still a common practice in most countries and deserves to be analyzed on that account.[63] Also, while government regulations may be more formal than other such prejudices against imports, their effects and problems of measurement are similar. Thus their analysis is actually representative of a much broader class of NTB.

Suppose, therefore, that an identifiable subset (government) of the demanders of a particular good show a preference for domestically produced goods as just described. That is, they undertake to buy domestic products unless imports can be obtained for, say, at least 10% cheaper. How will this affect the market? From the point of view of the subcategory of demanders that are subject to the requirement, decisions are made exactly as though there were a 10% tariff. Furthermore, if they do import, they actually pay only the lower price for the imports, and thus the implicit tariff revenue from the scheme stays within the demanding agency. Since the agency is part of the government, this completes the formal equivalence between a procurement regulation and a tariff.

However, there are two important differences, as well, between a procurement regulation and a tariff, and these have implications for empirical analysis.[64] First, unless the government is the only demander of the good in question, the implicit tariff here is levied on only a subset of demanders of the good within the country. Non-government demand continues to be allocated between domestic and imported goods on the basis of their actual prices. Thus when we aggregate the two groups of demanders to get the effect on the country's total demand for imports, the size of the implicit tariff will be smaller than 10%. That is, it will be approximately equal to 10% times the fraction that the government makes up of the total demand for the good. Also, depending on the nature of the good, the differential treatment of government and non-government demand may lead to a private sector response. That is, firms may increase their imports of the good and resell it to the government after only enough further processing to qualify for the preference for domestically produced goods. If this occurs, the implicit tariff can be reduced even closer to zero. Accordingly, the size of the procurement preference—10% in this example—may considerably overstate the extent of the true barrier that it imposes on international trade.

The second difficulty is that, contrary to what is the case with a tariff, the price on which import decisions are based is not observable. This means that if we use any of the conventional price-comparison methods of measuring NTBs, we may not succeed in capturing the effects of government procurement regulations where they exist. Even if domestically produced goods are perfect substitutes for imports and rise in price by the full amount of the procurement preference, an index of the good's price that includes imports will fail to include the elevated shadow price to which government demanders respond.

Calculations of the tariff equivalents of discriminatory government procurement policies for Canada are presented in Moroz and Brown (1987). Their methodology relied on what they call the "elasticity" approach, which we have discussed above in connection with figure 2.1 and quantity-impact measures of NTBs. The tariff equivalent (TE) here can be expressed as follows:

$$\text{(6)} \qquad TE = \frac{\Delta Q_m}{Q_m} \times \frac{(1+t)}{\eta}$$

where ΔQ_m is the change in imports induced by the NTB, Q_m is the pre-NTB level of imports, t is the nominal tariff rate, and η is the price elasticity of import demand.

Each industry can be divided into a government and private-sector submarket, and the TE for the government sub-market (TEG) is calculated as follows:

$$\text{(7)} \qquad TEG = \frac{APMP - APMG}{APMP} \times \frac{(1+t)}{\eta}$$

where APMP is the average propensity to import by the private sector and APMG is the average propensity to import by the government.

The foregoing equation assumes that imports and domestic goods are homogeneous, that markets are perfectly competitive, and that APMG and APMP would be identical if there were no discriminatory procurement policies present. It is important to note that private-sector purchases may be sensitive to procurement-induced price changes and that private firms may switch to imports if domestic market prices are increased with discriminatory government procurement. For relatively large economies, discriminatory procurement policies may not have a significant impact.[65,66]

Domestic Subsidies

A major source of complaint in international trade is the subsidization of domestic industry that puts foreign competitors at a perceived disadvantage. Domestic subsidies can take a variety of forms, ranging from credit guarantees to tax breaks on investment, and they are seldom as simple as the cash payments that we shall analyze here.[67] But this simple model can capture the essential features of their effects.

In figure 3.3 we show both the supply and demand on the domestic market, S_d and D_d, in the left panel and the implied excess supply and demand in the right panel.[68] The latter will appear either as the supply of exports, S_x, or the demand for imports, D_m, on the world market depending on the price that prevails there. Assume that a (specific) domestic subsidy equal to AB is now introduced, shifting the domestic supply curve down by the amount of the subsidy to S'_d. This in turn shifts the excess demand curve down also, and has effects in the world market that are analogous to either an export subsidy or a tariff, depending on the direction of trade. Indeed, if the world price happened to be between the old and new intersections of domestic supply and demand, then the subsidy would cause the country to switch from importing to exporting.

Now consider the problem of measuring the trade-distorting effects of this subsidy in a manner that will be comparable to other NTBs. Suppose for simplicity that the world price is fixed at p_w^0, so that the country imports the good, and these imports are reduced by the subsidy. The price on the domestic market will be the same as that on the world market, so that the price-impact measures discussed above will fail completely. Indeed, it is not clear that even conceptually there exists a true tariff equivalent of such a subsidy, since no tariff of any size will have the subsidy's effect of leaving unchanged, or even reducing, the domestic price.[69] On the other hand, the reduction in quantity of imports is analogous to that of tariffs and other NTBs, and regression measures that focus on quantities may pick it up.

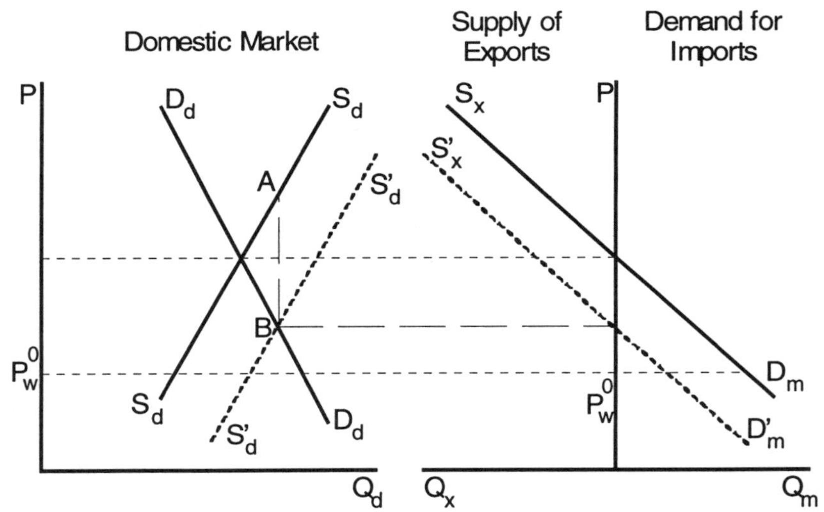

Figure 3.3
Effects of a Domestic Subsidy on
Export Supply and Import Demand

It will be tempting here to look at the domestic subsidy directly and, if its size can be determined, to use that as a measure of the distortion to trade. However it can be seen in figure 3.3 that this would be incorrect. The vertical shift of S_d is necessarily larger than that of the excess demand curve so long as domestic demand and supply are other than vertical and horizontal, respectively. Thus the size of the domestic subsidy provides an overestimate of the size of the implied NTB in terms of its effect on trade. This is true regardless of whether the subsidy serves to reduce imports or to stimulate exports.

Domestic subsidies are too important to ignore completely, however, and our recommendation is that they be measured in terms of their Output Subsidy Equivalent (OSE). This is defined as the direct subsidy to production that would have the same effect on output as the actual subsidy. Thus actual subsidies to output are just measured as their payments per unit of output and as a percent of cost. Subsidies to variable inputs, since these too reduce the marginal cost of additional output, are measured by their percentage cost reduction.[70] Subsidies that are paid over time and that appear to be unrelated to output may nonetheless have an effect on output if they permit a firm or plant to stay in operation instead of closing down. The OSE of such a subsidy can be measured by comparing the amount of the subsidy to costs and prices. One-time subsidies, such as a capital subsidy to finance an initial investment, also have effects on output by increasing firm capacity. Formulas for the OSEs of all of these types of subsidy are provided in appendix 3.

Domestic Content Requirements

These policies typically require that a certain fraction of domestic value added be included in goods sold on the domestic market. This introduces a straightforward trade barrier, to the extent that importers are forced to engage in further expensive processing that adds to their costs. The interesting feature of such a scheme is the way that it distorts the input decisions of producers. As a trade barrier, the increased cost of domestic processing is similar to a tariff, but the revenues that would be implicit in such a tariff are here dissipated in the form of production inefficiency.

Domestic content requirements can be analyzed in terms of the tradeoff between the value of production components that could be imported duty-free once the content requirement was met and the added cost of purchasing the production components from local sources. This is illustrated in figure 3.4, which we have adapted from Industry Commission (1994, p. 19) but interpreted somewhat differently. The line AC traces out the costs of purchasing locally under the content arrangement, with the components arrayed from the most competitive on the left to the least competitive on the right. The area under AC measures the value of domestically produced components. Assuming a small country with tariff, t, that applies to imported components, area E measures the tariff revenue saved by adhering to the content requirement. If the content requirement is adhered to, the firm saves the cost of area F but incurs the additional cost of area D. It will adhere to the requirement if area D is smaller than the sum of areas E+F.[71]

The effect of a domestic content requirement is further complicated because there may be restrictions on the import of the final product that uses both domestically produced and imported components. We shall say more on this below in discussing Australia's content requirements. In appendix 3 we provide a formula for the tariff equivalent for a domestic content requirement in terms of a general benefit provided to the firm in return for compliance. The case of figure 3.4, where the benefit takes the special form of tariff remission on remaining imported inputs, then follows as a special case.

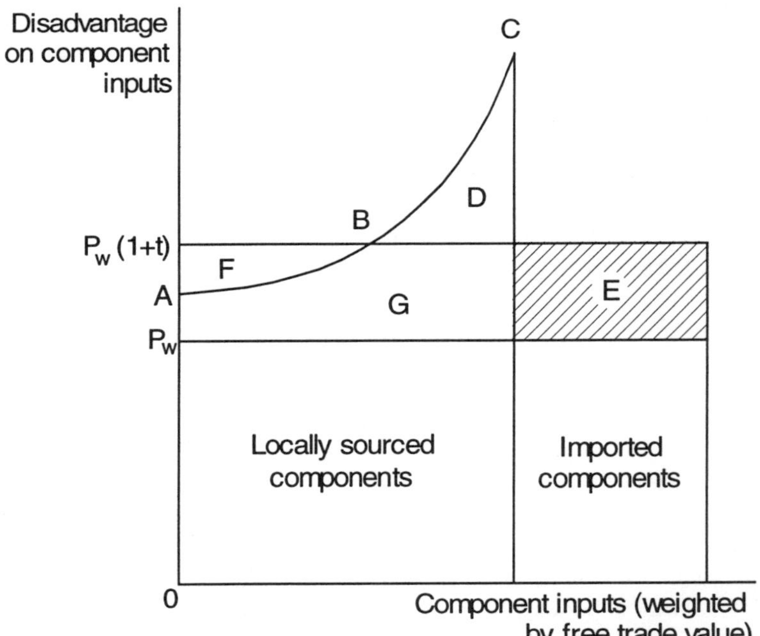

Source: Industry Commission (1994, p. 19)

Figure 3.4
Domestic Content Requirements

Antidumping and Countervailing Duty Measures

Antidumping (AD) duties are intended to offset actions by foreign firms that export for a price that is below the price in their domestic market or below cost. Countervailing duties (CVD) are intended to counteract foreign government subsidies for exports or domestic production.

Once imposed, AD duties and CVDs are simply tariffs and need no special form of analysis. However, an established procedure for imposing such duties will itself distort behavior in international trade even if the duties themselves never have to be levied.[72] That is, the procedure may serve as a signal to foreign producers to raise their prices to an announced level and thus charge higher prices than they otherwise would in hopes of avoiding AD or CVD penalties. Given that dumping and foreign subsidies are an accepted justification for intervention worldwide, it will be very difficult empirically to determine what price exporters would have charged if this were not the case.

There are, however, several cases in which it may be possible to do better than using only the actual duties collected as a measure of the trade restricting effects of AD and CVD laws. In AD cases that are resolved by a settlement rather than by a duty, the settlement itself may provide such a measure. If the settlement is a "price undertaking," then that price, in comparison to previous prices, measures its tariff equivalent. Similarly, a "quantity undertaking" can be translated to a price effect using an import elasticity. Somewhat more generally, if a particular country and sector is suspected to be unusually prone to AD actions, a price comparison similar to those mentioned above for VERs may indicate the effect. All of this is spelled out in somewhat more detail in appendix 3.

An indication of the major users of AD and CVD measures among GATT signatories for 1988–1993 is given in table 3.7. The numbers of AD and CVD measures in force by country and directed at exporting countries for 1990–1993 are shown in table 3.8 and 3.9. Table 3.10 contains a sectoral breakdown of the number of AD and CVD measures. These data are useful in identifying the country and sectoral coverage of AD and CVD measures, but they are subject to the same criticism made above of frequency ratios, which is that they do not convey any information on the economic impacts involved.

Customs Valuation Procedures

Announced levels of tariffs can be misleading if they are levied against a base of an artificially elevated price. This is easily dealt with empirically, however, by comparing tariff revenues with the value of imports and thus inferring what the true tariff percentage must have been. More difficult, however, is the problem that arises when traders do not have a clear idea of the valuation procedure that will be used, well in advance of making their trading decisions. In that case trade can be reduced far beyond what any simple measure of tariff revenues or prices could indicate. Both cases are dealt with briefly in appendix

3, the latter by again comparing export prices to prices charged by the same exporter in other markets.

A further problem arises in dealing with transfer pricing by multinational enterprises (MNEs) since intra-firm prices may be under- or overstated depending on how MNEs seek to minimize their global tax payments. In these circumstances what is needed is some measure of an "arm's-length" price as a reference that can then be compared to the observed import and domestic

TABLE 3.7. Percentage Share of Anti-Dumping (AD) and Countervailing Duty (CVD) Measures in Force by GATT Signatories, 1988-1993

Country	AD Measures	CVD Measures
United States	43.5%	68.0%
European Union-12	26.0	0.5
Canada	13.4	20.5
Australia	7.7	5.2
Mexico	3.4	0.0
Brazil	1.5	4.6
Chile	0.0	1.0
Other	4.5	0.2
Total	**100.0%**	**100.0%**

Source: Adapted from Chapman and Lee (1995, p. 13).

TABLE 3.8. Number of Anti-Dumping (AD) and Countervailing Duty (CVD) Measures in Force by GATT Signatories, 1990-1993

Measures/Country	1990	1991	1992	1993
AD Measures				
United States	201	216	267	304
European Union-12	137	144	159	150
Canada	78	69	73	85
Australia	24	30	44	76
Mexico	6	19	23	28
Brazil	0	2	9	23
Other	12	19	33	38
CVD Measures				
United States	94	87	93	122
European Union-12	--	1	--	2
Canada	31	30	29	29
Australia	1	5	12	12
Brazil	--	1	13	13
Chile	--	2	4	0
New Zealand	--	--	--	1

Source: Adapted from Chapman and Lee (1995, p. 14).

TABLE 3.9. Number and Share of Anti-Dumping (AD) and Countervailing Duty (CVD) Measures Directed at Exporting Countries, 1990-1993

	Number of measures				Share
	1990	1991	1992	1993	1990-1993
AD Measures					
Other	173	176	233	268	32.8%
European Union-12	67	68	74	96	13.4
Japan	79	81	86	86	14.6
China	32	48	62	74	9.5
Korea	28	34	40	48	6.6
United States	18	27	33	48	5.6
Taiwan	26	29	36	37	5.6
Brazil	19	21	28	30	4.3
Canada	16	15	16	17	2.8
Thailand	..	..	..	..	2.1
Mexico	..	..	..	..	1.6
Argentina	..	..	..	..	1.0
Total	..	..	..	..	**100.0%**
CVD Measures					
Other	37	42	42	54	29.6%
European Union-12	43	45	64	73	38.7
Japan	..	..	..	..	0.2
Korea	1	1	1	3	1.0
United States	..	..	..	..	0.3
Taiwan	1	1	1	1	0.7
Brazil	11	11	11	13	7.9
Canada	7	3	6	6	3.8
Thailand	8	9	10	11	6.5
Mexico	8	4	5	5	3.8
Argentina	10	10	11	13	7.6
Total	..	..	..	..	**100.0%**

Not reported.

Source: Adapted from Chapman and Lee (1995, pp. 15-16).

TABLE 3.10. Number and Share of Anti-Dumping (AD) and Countervailing Duty (CVD) Measures in Force by Product, 1990-1993

	Number of Measures				Share
	1990	1991	1992	1993	1990-1993
AD Measures					
Chemicals	94	110	143	155	22.1%
Primary metals	77	88	126	178	20.7
Electrical products	61	76	74	74	12.6
Fabricated metals	55	47	49	53	9.0
Textiles	26	28	41	41	6.0
Food	17	19	22	32	4.0
Printing and publishing	20	23	22	24	3.9
Leather products	..	..	..	..	3.1
Machinery	..	..	..	..	3.1
Agricultural products	..	..	..	..	2.1
Clothing	..	..	..	..	0.5

	Number of Measures				Share
	1990	1991	1992	1993	1990-1993
Other	108	108	131	147	13.0
Total	..	..	..	..	100.0%
CVD Measures					
Clothing	7	6	7	9	52.0
Food	46	49	70	67	39.9
Primary metals	27	25	26	50	22.0
Textiles	10	12	11	13	7.9
Agricultural products	12	11	10	10	7.4
Fabricated metals	10	10	10	11	7.0
Chemicals	3	3	3	2	1.9%
Machinery	..	..	..	..	1.7
Electrical products	..	..	..	..	0.7
Leather products	2	2	2	2	1.4
Printing and publishing					-
Other	9	8	12	13	5.2
Total	..	..	..	..	**100.0%**

Not reported.
Source: Adapted from Chapman and Lee (1995, pp. 17-18).

prices in the importing country. While the customs authorities may themselves seek information on how imports by MNE affiliates should be valued in levying import duties, it is not altogether clear whether such information is public knowledge. Given the importance of intra-firm MNE trade and the incentives for minimizing tax payments, the existence of transfer pricing raises a host of difficult problems in measuring border protection that are deserving of greater attention.

Technical Barriers to Trade[73]

There is widespread reliance on standards, technical regulations, and certification systems that have been developed to enhance the availability of information and to reduce uncertainties about the quality characteristics of goods and services purchased by firms and households. Standards are generally voluntarily defined by business groups or nongovernmental standardization organizations, whereas technical regulations are legally binding. Certification systems are intended to assure compliance with existing standards or regulations.

To the extent that standards, technical regulations, and certification systems differ across countries, they may act as technical barriers to the flow of trade. What is important, however, is not whether they differ per se, but whether the standards are applied differentially between domestic and foreign goods. The use of price comparisons in assessing inter-country differences in standards may thus be of limited use, since these price differences may not in themselves reflect barriers to trade. What is needed accordingly is information provided by technical experts who are familiar with the details of the standards, regulations, and certification systems applied to particular products or processes. In particular, it may be possible to construct estimates of the added costs involved when: (1) higher standards are applied to imported as compared to domestic goods; (2) regulations are enforced more stringently on imports; and (3) imports are subjected to more cumbersome and costly certification procedures. These considerations are taken into account in the discussion of measuring technical barriers to trade in appendix 3.

Conclusion

Our analysis of NTB-specific problems of measurement in this chapter suggests two general conclusions.

First, the implementation of most NTBs provides only relatively little direct information about their size, and the information available is often misleading. We have seen this with procurement regulations and subsidies, where the formal percentages of preference or subsidy may overstate the true size of their price effects on trade, and this is likely to be true of other NTBs as well. The reason is that markets have an uncanny ability to circumvent attempts to intervene in them, and policies—though often very distorting in unintended ways—seldom achieve the direct effects for which they were intended.[74]

Second, attempts to infer the presence and size of NTBs from observed price differentials between domestic markets and world or foreign markets are fraught with difficulty and will often miss or underestimate many NTBs. We saw this even for relatively straightforward NTBs such as quotas, and the theme was repeated through all of the other examples that we have looked at in this chapter. Thus we remain cautious about the usefulness of price-comparison measures of NTBs except in those cases where the nature and local circumstances of a specific NTB are well understood to be appropriate for this methodology.

On the other hand, while measures based on quantities of trade often appear preferable to price comparisons at a conceptual level, the fact remains that we seldom have a good enough understanding of the quantitative determinants of trade to make these measurements. Therefore price comparisons are likely to be the only viable option for measuring most NTBs. We have outlined here how such comparisons may be undertaken in the various cases, and we provide more detail in appendix 3.

General Methods for Measuring the Effects of NTBs

We have concentrated thus far on issues of measuring the *size* of NTBs. Our discussion would not be complete without also mentioning how NTB measures, once they have been obtained, may be used to assess the effects of NTBs on economic variables of interest, such as domestic resource allocation, trade and economic welfare. We have already discussed calculation of the nominal rate of assistance (NRA), which is commonly used in calculating measures of *effective rates of protection* (ERP) and *effective rates of assistance* (ERA). Measures of ERP and ERA, as will be indicated below, are used to indicate how the structure of net border and domestic incentives may affect the allocation of labor, capital, and land among the sectors of an economy. We shall also discuss calculation of the *Trade Restrictiveness Index* (TRI), which is another method for measuring the effects of the structure of trade policies. Finally, reference will be made to the use of applied general equilibrium (AGE) models that are designed to simulate the economic effects of changes in existing border and domestic policies.

Effective Rates of Protection (ERPs) and Effective Rates of Assistance (ERAs)

Nominal tariff rates and nominal measures of the ad valorem equivalents of NTBs are valuable tools for documenting the presence of trade barriers and for measuring their size on a consistent basis. They are of little use directly, however, for indicating the effects of trade barriers, even in the industries that they ostensibly protect. A major reason is that they refer only to protection of outputs and thus do not take into account the effects of such nominal protection on input costs. Corden (1966) provides the classic reference for the rationale and calculation of ERPs as a means of determining the effects of the entire structure of protection on resource allocation. In order to calculate ERPs, data are needed on both nominal protection in all sectors and the interindustry (input-output) structure of the economy. These data then permit calculation of how sectoral value added is changed due to the structure of protection. Calculation of ERAs is a broader undertaking, since it involves measures of the size of both border and domestic incentives, and it also allows, like the ERP, for input-output interactions.

Trade Restrictiveness Index (TRI)

The TRI, which was developed originally by Anderson and Neary (1991, 1994), is intended to provide a comprehensive measure of NTBs in terms of their welfare effects.[75] An advantage of the TRI is that it provides a single number that characterizes the overall effects of a country's trade policies that apply to a particular aggregate of goods under general equilibrium conditions. But in order to calculate the TRI, information is needed on the prices of imports being protected, world prices, measures of tariff equivalents of products to be included, and measures of own-price elasticity of demand. The TRI may thus require almost as much information about an economy as would be needed for a complete applied general equilibrium (AGE) model. From the standpoint of the present study, which is focused on measuring the size of NTBs, the resultant measures can be directly useful in calculating the TRI.

But because the TRI provides primarily a measure of economic welfare due to changes in trade policies, it seems disadvantageous as compared to a full scale AGE model, which typically would provide economy-wide detail on sectoral changes in trade, output, employment, and other variables of interest.

Applied General Equilibrium (AGE) Model Measures

AGE models provide the most comprehensive framework for quantitative assessments of the economic effects of changes in both trade and domestic policies. As mentioned above, the calculation of ERAs makes it possible to obtain a single overall measure of the net incentives furnished by the structure of existing policies under conditions of partial equilibrium. However, since ERAs do not take into account interactions between industries and countries, they may not provide an accurate indication of how resource allocation and economic welfare may change as trade and domestic policies are changed. Because the TRI is derived under general equilibrium assumptions, it also may be preferable to measurements of ERAs. But if one is interested in the economy-wide impacts of policy changes at the sectoral level, construction of an AGE model should be the preferred methodology.

AGE models have come to be widely used in the past twenty-five years or so especially for analyzing the consequences of trade liberalization and changes in domestic tax structures. Such models can be constructed using a single country multisectoral framework in which trade is treated in the aggregate.[76] There are also numerous multisector, multicountry AGE models in current use.[77]

While AGE models have the advantage of providing comprehensive measurement of the effects of changes in policies, these models require a substantial amount of sectoral data and parameters. Also, to the extent that one is concerned with analysis of selected NTBs, partial equilibrium measures may suffice. In any case, since our present concern is to review existing methodologies for measuring the *size* of NTBs, we can leave aside considerations of which type of framework may be best suited for using such estimates in evaluating the effects of reducing or removing NTBs. Regardless of whether one opts to calculate ERPs or ERAs, to compute the TRI, or to construct a complete AGE model, all of these frameworks require comprehensive and accurate measurements of the NTBs themselves before any calculation of effects can begin.

CHAPTER 4

Overview and Assessment of Economy-Wide Estimates of NTBs in Selected OECD Countries

In this chapter, we review and evaluate the methodology and results of selected country studies and related materials prepared by member countries of the OECD Pilot Group that seek to measure the size of NTBs and other forms of government assistance across different sectors of individual economies. This is not intended to be a complete survey of this literature, but only an illustrative sample. Focus is primarily on the OECD Pilot Group studies and related sources that were mentioned in those studies or that we had dealt with in our previous work.

Australia

It seems fair to say that more work has been done in Australia in measuring NTBs and other forms of assistance than in any other major country. The focus of this work has been on the assistance to all industries provided not only by tariffs and other trade barriers, but by various domestic policies as well. Nonetheless there is a wealth of information in the Australian sources that deals explicitly with NTBs. We report a sample of results for various kinds of assistance, among which many of the NTBs we have addressed in this study appear prominently.

Forms of Assistance

The forms of assistance provided to Australian manufacturing are shown in table 4.1 for selected years, from 1983–84 to 2000–01 (projected). It is evident that tariffs are the dominant form of assistance both to outputs and materials and that the absolute amounts are to become significantly smaller as projected for 1996–97 and 2000–01, reflecting the continuing tariff reductions to be carried out. The forms of assistance used for Australian agriculture for selected years, from 1983–84 to 1992–93, are indicated in table 4.2. Domestic pricing arrangements are the chief form of assistance to agricultural outputs, while adjustment assistance, agricultural research, and income tax concessions are the major forms of assistance to value adding factors. Tariffs on inputs, shown with a negative sign, represent in effect a tax on the material and plant and machinery used in Australian agriculture.

TABLE 4.1. Australia: Assistance to Manufacturing by Form, 1983-84 to 2000-01[a] (A$ Million)

	1983-84	1989-90	1992-93	1996-97	2000-01
Assistance to outputs					
Tariffs[b]	8205	13671	12725	6629	5562
Quantitative import restrictions	1248	505	56	..	..
Bounties[c]	139	298	124	50	47
Export incentives[c]	219	241	273	285	285
Assistance to materials[d]					
Tariffs[b]	–3604	–5064	–4918	–2624	–2274
Quantitative import restrictions	–493	–94	–49	--	--
Excise taxes	–8	–97	–100	–100	–100
Assistance to value adding factors[e]	..	..	58	8	8

- Nil.

.. Less than $0.5 million.

a Estimates for 1983-84 and 1989-90 are in 1983-84 and 1989-90 prices, respectively. Estimates for 1992-93, 1996-97 and 2000-01 are, respectively, the sum of the gross subsidy equivalents and the tax on materials for individual industries, classified according to form of assistance. The summation of these amounts across industries will exceed the actual total for the sector due to some of the outputs of industries being used as intermediate inputs by other industries within the sector.

b Includes relatively minor amounts of assistance from domestic pricing arrangements for certain agricultural commodities. Figures are net of the savings from concessional entry of imported materials under certain policy by-laws, commercial tariff concession orders, duty drawback and by-law for exports.

c Except for the base years 1983-84 and 1989-90 the estimates presented in this table do not represent the actual bounty and export incentive payments in each year. The estimates measure the assistance afforded by the current rates of bounty and export incentives in each year using fixed 1983-84 and 1989-90 production patterns respectively.

d Figures for assistance to materials were reported as positive numbers in the source, apparently in error.

e The Industry Commission's new series of estimates includes, for the first time, some assistance to value-adding factors; namely certain capital grants and concessional loans for TCF industries.

Source: Adapted from Industry Commission (1995, table 4.2).

TABLE 4.2. Australia: Assistance to Agriculture by Form, 1982-83 to 1992-93[a] (A$ Million)

	1983-84	1989-90	1992-93
Assistance to outputs	**730**	**584**	**633**
Domestic pricing arrangements[b]	555	402	393
Export inspection[c]	55	59	9
Local content schemes	23	26	30
Marketing support	22	25	50
Tariffs	62	42	28
Other	13	30	123
Assistance to value adding factors	**331**	**435**	**355**
Adjustment assistance	29	72	106
Agricultural research	99	144	167
Income tax concessions[d]	96	205	78
Other	107	14	4
Assistance to inputs	**-301**	**-237**	**-166**
Tariffs on material	-158	-118	-105
Tariffs on plant and machinery[e]	-204	-129	-66
Other	61	10	5

a This table covers total assistance to the agricultural sector. A small amount of assistance is provided through general measures (e.g. income tax concessions) to activities for which nominal and effective rates have not been estimated.

b These estimates include the effects of any import restrictions which enable the domestic price to exceed the landed duty-free price of competing imports (e.g. tariffs on dried vine fruits and sugar).

c Since 1989-90 assistance has been based on shortfalls from 100 percent cost recovery.

d Includes assistance provided to primary producers through the income tax averaging provisions and the immediate deductibility of capital expenditure on water storage and farm reticulation systems (S.75B) and land degradation measures (S.75D). In 1984-85, minor assistance was also provided through the immediate deductibility of expenditure on fences for the control of bovine brucellosis and tuberculosis (S.75C). No assistance has been allocated to the agricultural sector by the optional special depreciation rates (20 percent prime cost per annum, or for expenditure incurred from 20 July 1982 to 19 May 1983, 33.3 percent) following the availability to all taxpayers of optional depreciation rates of 20 percent or 33.3 percent prime cost per annum from 20 July 1982.

e The additional costs incurred due to assistance raising the prices of inputs. The latest series includes the effect of tariffs on materials used in non-traded inputs.

Source: Industry Commission (1995, table A5.1).

Price Comparisons

We have just noted that tariffs were by far the major form of assistance provided to Australian manufacturing. While quantitative import restrictions have been important, especially for the textile, clothing, and footwear (TCF) industries and for the passenger motor vehicle (PMV) industry, these restrictions were removed for PMV as of April 1988 and for TCF as of April 1993, according to Industry Commission (1995, p. 75). While the Industry Commission had used comparisons between import and domestic prices for TCF prior to the 1980s, they shifted subsequently to using information on the quota premiums based on information derived from official auctioning of the quotas. This methodology was also applied to PMV. The bids for the quota sales, according to Industry Commission (1995, p. 79), were in terms of an ad valorem tariff rate that the bidder was willing to pay in addition to the base tariff rate already existing. Estimates of these combined base plus tender premiums for a number of individual categories of TCF and PMV are given in table 4.3 for 1982, 1988, and 1992. In interpreting these estimates, it should be noted that average clothing and footwear tariffs were 36, 40, and 43 percent while the average tariffs on transport equipment were 13, 18, and 10 percent in the respective years. The ad valorem equivalents of the import quotas were thus sizable for many of the products listed.

TABLE 4.3. Australia: Base Tariffs Plus Tender Premiums for Textiles, Clothing, and Footwear (TCF) and Passenger Motor Vehicles (PMV), 1982, 1988, and 1992 (Percent)

Tender category descriptions[a]	1982	1988	1992[b]
Knitted or crocheted coats, jumpers, cardigans, sweaters and the like, tube tops	84	60	61
Shirts and blouses and knitted or crocheted tops	86	na	na
Knitted shirts and blouses	n	205	74
Woven shirts and blouses	na	122	66
Woven coats and jackets; sets of men's garments, including suits	87	80	58
Leather coats and jackets	55	67	60
Trousers, jeans and overalls	70	62	64
Shorts and male swimwear	62	50	68
Women's, girls' and infants' swimwear	75	50	51
Certain children's wear	71	51	54
Men's woven pyjamas	74	na	na
Dresses, dressing gowns, adult nightdresses and nightshirts, other outergarments and other sleepwear	74	na	na
Dresses, other outwear, pyjamas	na	51	62
Other undergarments for men and boys; other undergarments for women, girls and infants	90	87	70
Brassieres; corsets, girdles and the like	84	50	61
Garments of plastic materials, of rubber, or the like	60	55	51
Tights and pantyhose less than 4.4 tex	76	126	51
Socks and the like; tights pantyhose 4.4 tex or more	76	50	59
Footwear with leather uppers	71	63	50
Other footwear	90	65	41
Parts for footwear	55	63	10
Terry toweling, towels, babies' napkins and the like	81	80	61
Bed linen, including quilt covers and bed ruffles	60	56	52
Fabric suitable for use as bed sheeting and the like, or in the making up of bed linen	48	72	37
Woven fabric of man-made fibres	70	72	45
Curtains	50	40	--
Sleeping bags having a customs value not exceeding $30 each	25	25	--
Motor vehicles	na	57.5	--

-- Nil.
na Not applicable.
a The descriptions for some categories changed on 1 January 1988 and again in March 1989.
b In 1992, the base duty rates were reduced in preparation for the removal of quota in the following year. For most items, the rates reduced from 55 percent to 51 percent. Footwear with leather uppers and other footwear were reduced from 45 percent to 41 percent. Parts for footwear were reduced from 35 percent to 10 percent. Fabric suitable for use as bedsheeting and Woven fabric of man made fibres were reduced from 40 percent to 37 percent.
Source: Adapted from Industry Commission (1995, table A3.1).

We should also mention that, if information is available, both price-comparison and quota-auction price measures can be constructed and compared. This has been done in Australia. In Industry Commission (1994, p.8), reference was made to a survey by the Australian Retailers Association of the so-called price disadvantage of Australian clothing items that were both produced domestically and imported under quota. The results of the price-disadvantage survey are presented together with estimates of the average quota tender premium between 1982 and 1986 in table 4.4.[1] While several of the estimates are fairly close, there are a number that diverge noticeably. This suggests that it may be useful to carry out more than one approach in measuring NTBs, but problems will no doubt arise in assuring that the prices of like products are in fact being compared.

Nominal Rates of Assistance

The average nominal rates of assistance (NRA) on outputs for Australian two-digit ASIC manufacturing sectors are given in table 4.5 for selected years, from 1971–72 to 2000–01 (projected). It can be seen that the NRAs have declined considerably over the years shown, reflecting the aforementioned reductions in Australian tariffs and other supports. On the basis of the projections for 2000–01, the highest NRAs are: clothing and footwear, 19%; transport equipment, 10%; fabricated metals, 9%; and textiles, 6%. The NRA for total manufacturing is projected to be 3%. The average nominal rates of assistance on materials (NRM) for Australian manufacturing are shown in table 4.6. Again, the NRMs can be seen to have fallen noticeably since 1971–72 and are projected to decline considerably more by 2000–01. The average NRAs for the main Australian agricultural activities are given in table 4.7, for 1983–84 to 1992–93. The intensive livestock and horticulture activities have the highest NRAs, but they have declined markedly over the period indicated.

Effective Rates of Assistance

The definition of the ERA used in Australia is given in appendix 2 together with an illustrative calculation of the ERA for the Australian iron and steel industry for the mid–1980s. Estimates of ERAs for Australian manufacturing sectors for selected years, from 1971–72 to 2000–01 (projected) are shown in table 4.8. Comparison of these ERAs with the NRAs and NRMs for Australia listed in tables 4.5 and 4.6 above provides an indication of the effects of the structure of net incentives. Thus, for example, the ERAs projected for 2000–01 are: clothing and footwear, 34%; motor vehicles and parts, 19%; and textiles, 17%. These compare to the projected NRAs in table 4.5 which were 19%, 10%, and 6%, respectively. The ERAs can be seen in table 4.9 to have declined significantly since the 1970s as the net assistance to the individual sectors has been and will continue to be reduced. The average ERA for all manufacturing is projected to fall to 3% in 2000–01. The ERAs for the main activities of Australian agriculture are noted in table 4.9. The highest ERA in 1992–93 was 32% for Intensive Livestock. For total agriculture, the ERA was 11% in 1992–93. The comparable NRAs were 10% and 4%, respectively.

TABLE 4.4. Australia: Comparisons of Industry Commission and Survey Estimates of Clothing NTBs for the Mid-1980s (Percent)

Quota category no.	Description	Tariff Equivalent 1982-86[a] Base Tariff Plus Tender	Price Dis-advantage[b] 1984
101, 101H	Knitted coats, jumpers, cardigans, sweaters, tube tops etc.	96	98
102	Knitted shirts and blouses	108	107
103, 103H	Woven shirts and blouses	108	127
104	Woven coats	106	107
105	Leather coats and jackets	71	112
106	Men's suits and coats	106	91
107	Trousers, jeans and overalls	89	138
108	Shorts and male swimwear	80	131
109, 109H	Female swimwear	106	131
110, 110H	Dresses, dressing gowns etc., adult night-dresses	91	91
111	Certain children's wear	100	120
112	Men's woven pyjamas	85	81
113, 113H	Other outerwear	91	85
114	Undergarments, men's	80	146
115	Undergarments, women's	80	61
116	Brassieres	129	151
117	Waist-encircling foundation	129	102
118[c]	Plastic/rubber apparel	72	62
119	Pantyhose	66	117
120	Socks and tights	66	--
121	Footwear with leather uppers	89	66
122	Footwear with non-leather uppers	110	--
123[c]	Parts for footwear	71	--
124, 124H	Towelling and towelling products	86	--
125	Bed linen	53	--
126	Curtains	44	--
127	Sleeping bags	29	--
128[d]	Cotton sheeting	12-52	--
129	Woven fabric of man-made fibre	78	--

a Base tariff plus average tender premiums between 1982 and 1986.

b Estimates prepared by the Australian Retailer's Association.

c Value-based quota categories.

d Category 128 is comprised of three tariff items with differing rates of duty. The tariff equivalents of these items are:

55.09.61252%

55.09.61135%

55.09.61312%

Source: Industry Commission (1994, pp. 14-15).

TABLE 4.5. Australia: Average Nominal Rates of Assistance on Outputs (NRA) for Manufacturing, 1971-72 to 2000-01 (Percent)

ASIC	Sector	1971-72	1974-75	1977-78	1983-84	1989-90	2000-01
21-22	Food, Beverages, and Tobacco	11	9	16	8	5	3
23	Textiles	25	20	24	23	19	6
24	Clothing and Footwear	49	42	64	78	63	19
25	Wood, Wood Products, and Furniture	20	14	12	14	12	4
26	Paper, Paper Products, Printing and Publishing	28	17	15	12	7	2
27	Chemicals, Petroleum and Coal Products	21	9	11	4	2	1
28	Non-metallic Metal Products	11	7	4	3	3	1
29	Basic Metal Products	14	8	6	6	4	2
31	Fabricated Metal Products	36	25	20	17	13	4
32	Transport Equipment	33	27	33	39	24	9
323	Motor Vehicles and Parts	34	29	38	51	28	10
33	Other Machinery and Equipment	32	21	16	17	15	4
34	Miscellaneous Manufacturing	29	21	23	19	14	5
21-34	**Total Manufacturing**	**22**	**15**	**15**	**13**	**9**	**3**

Note: See notes to table 11.
Source: Adapted from Industry Commission (1995, tables A6.1 and A6.4).

TABLE 4.6. Australia: Average Nominal Rates of Assistance on Materials (NRM) for Manufacturing, 1971-72 to 2000-01 (Percent)

ASIC	Sector	1971-72	1974-75	1977-78	1983-84	1989-90	2000-01
21-22	Food, Beverages, and Tobacco	6	3	3	8	5	3
23	Textiles	13	10	11	8	5	3
24	Clothing and Footwear	22	18	26	8	7	2
25	Wood, Wood Products, and Furniture	17	9	7	10	8	3
26	Paper, Paper Products, Printing and Publishing	8	7	7	8	5	2
27	Chemicals, Petroleum and Coal Products	13	4	6	2	1	--
28	Non-metallic Metal Products	7	3	3	3	2	1
29	Basic Metal Products	5	2	4	5	2	1
31	Fabricated Metal Products	17	13	12	11	8	4
32	Transport Equipment	24	18	25	26	14	6
323	Motor Vehicles and Parts	27	19	27	29	15	6
33	Other Machinery and Equipment	24	17	13	13	11	3
34	Miscellaneous Manufacturing	26	15	16	14	9	3
21-34	**Total Manufacturing**	**13**	**8**	**9**	**8**	**5**	**2**

Notes: See notes to table 11.

Source: Adapted from Industry Commission (1995, tables A6.2 and A6.5).

TABLE 4.7. Australia: Average Nominal Rates of Assistance (NRA) for Agriculture, 1983-84 to 1992-93 (Percent)

Activity[a]	1983-84	1989-90	1992-93
Horticulture	12	4	4
Extensive cropping	2	1	1
Extensive irrigation and high rainfall crops	8	3	2
Extensive grazing	2	1	2
Intensive livestock	23	11	10
Total Agriculture	**6**	**3**	**4**

[a]Activity average. For detailed commodity NRAs, see source below.

Source: Industry Commission (1995, table A5.2).

ERAs are subject to a number of critical assumptions,[1] which, if violated, could result in inaccurate measurements. Some of the difficulties may be moderated to the extent that the ERAs are measured regularly over time and data bases are continually updated. Nonetheless, it is important to bear in mind that ERAs are partial equilibrium measures of the net incentives due to the structure of assistance. If one wishes to analyze the economy-wide effects of these incentives, it will then be necessary to have a general equilibrium model that can take into account the various interactions that may occur both within and between individual sectors as well as interactions with major trading partners. Thus, for our purposes, it is only the *direct* effects on domestic prices that matter in defining the tariff equivalents of NTBs. To include the effects on barriers in one industry on input prices in another industry would blur the meaning of tariff equivalents for individual industries since they would include effects from other industries' barriers. By calculating only the direct effects on prices, the resulting measures can be incorporated into other conceptual frameworks that take input-output relationships into account.

Domestic Content Requirements

Australia has maintained domestic content requirements for automobiles and tobacco. The automobile industry was formerly subject to an 85 percent content requirement. As noted in Industry Commission (1995, p. 22), the disadvantage on locally sourced content in 1980, as reflected in both local component production and vehicle assembly, was estimated to be about 80 percent. This content arrangement was discontinued as of January 1, 1989.

The content requirement for tobacco used in producing cigarettes and other tobacco products was set at 50 percent by weight for use of locally produced tobacco leaves. Once the content requirement was met, tobacco leaves could be imported at concessional rates. Because there were marketing arrangements designed to assist the domestic tobacco industry, it is difficult to distinguish the effects of the content requirement and the marketing arrangements. What was done then was to make price comparisons between domestically produced and imported leaf products in order to calculate the price disadvantages involved. These measures were then interpreted as tariff equivalents. During the period from 1989–90 to 1992–93, the average price disadvantage was around 40 percent. Details are given in table 4.10. The content requirement for tobacco leaf was discontinued as of January 1, 1995.

Canada

Price Comparisons

Estimates of NTBs for Canada are reviewed in Sheikh and Beausejour (1995). These estimates refer primarily to the 1980s and were used as inputs in the negotiation of the Canada-U.S. Free Trade Agreement that was implemented at the beginning of 1989. The most detailed work on Canadian NTBs was done by Moroz and Brown (1987), with updating especially by Campbell and Cossette (1994).[2] Estimates of nonzero sectoral tariff equivalents of quantitative restrictions for 1980–1985 are provided in table 4.11. It is evident that the highest tariff equivalents were experienced in a number of agricultural and food products sectors, footwear, and clothing. The calculations involved were done mainly based on price comparisons. Some estimates were also made using the "cost-push" method for wheat flour and poultry products.[3]

Government Procurement

We noted above that Moroz and Brown (1987) calculated tariff equivalents for discriminatory government procurement. They included federal non-defense, and provincial purchases.[4] Results for selected sectors are listed in table 4.12 for cases in which the tariff equivalent exceeded one percent. The estimated import price elasticities for these sectors are also given in table 4.12. The ad valorem equivalents ranged from 1.1% for petroleum products to 10.6% for scientific equipment. In our earlier discussion of methods for measuring specific NTBs, we discussed the difficulties in measuring the size of procurement barriers and the methodology that Moroz and Brown used which was based on the "elasticity" approach. Their calculations should therefore be considered suggestive rather than definitive.

TABLE 4.8. Australia: Average Effective Rates of Assistance (ERA) for Manufacturing, 1971-72 to 2000-01 (Percent)

ASIC	Sector	1971-72	1974-75	1977-78	1983-84	1989-90	2000-01
21-22	Food, Beverages, and Tobacco	19	21	10	6	4	7
23	Textiles	45	39	47	69	53	17
24	Clothing and Footwear	86	87	141	227	113	34
25	Wood, Wood Products, and Furniture	23	18	18	18	15	4
26	Paper, Paper Products, Printing and Publishing	52	31	24	16	9	2
27	Chemicals, Petroleum and Coal Products	32	23	19	12	8	3
28	Non-metallic Metal Products	14	11	5	4	4	2
29	Basic Metal Products	29	16	10	10	9	4
31	Fabricated Metal Products	58	39	30	25	19	4
32	Transport Equipment	50	45	48	65	37	13
323	Motor Vehicles and Parts	49	‘54	73	129	52	19
33	Other Machinery and Equipment	44	24	20	22	19	6
34	Miscellaneous Manufacturing	32	27	30	26	20	7
21-34	**Total Manufacturing**	**35**	**27**	**23**	**22**	**15**	**5**

Note: See notes to table 11.
Source: Adapted from Industry Commission (1995, table 4.1).

TABLE 4.9. Australia: Average Effective Rates of Assistance (ERA) for Agriculture, 1983-84 to 1992-93 (Percent)

Activity[a]	1983-84	1989-90	1992-93
Horticulture	22	8	8
Extensive cropping	1	2	4
Extensive irrigation and high rainfall crops	11	10	5
Extensive grazing	7	3	8
Intensive livestock	59	32	32
Total Agriculture	**12**	**7**	**11**

[a]Activity average. For detailed commodity ERAs, see source below.
Source: Industry Commission (1995, table A5.3).

TABLE 4.10. Australia: Price Disadvantage (Green Leaf) by Tobacco Leaf Type in Australia, 1989-90 to 1992-93 (Percent)

Leaf type	1989-90	1990-91	1991-92	1992-93	Average
Tips	27	30	34	71	40
Subleaf	43	34	35	56	42
Leaf	32	31	32	59	38
Cutters	55	41	34	63	48
Lugs	89	55	52	82	69

Notes: The price disadvantage is calculated as the difference between the domestic and import substitution price divided by the import substitution price. The four-year average reported is the simple arithmetic average over the period.
Source: Industry Commission (1995, p. 26).

TABLE 4.11. Canada: Non-zero Estimates of Sectoral Tariff Equivalents of Quantitative Restrictions, 1980-1985 (Percent)

Sector	Tariff Equivalent
Agricultural and food products	
Agriculture	12.6
Poultry	11.5
Dairy products	37.7
Feed mills	0.8
Flour and breakfast cereals	5.7
Distilleries and breweries	41.2
Wineries	52.3
Leather products and clothing	
Leather tanning	0.1
Leather footwear	5.1
Other knitting	3.5
Clothing	15.0
Other furniture	0.1
Metal products	
Smelting	0.1
Boiler and plate works	0.7

Fabricated structural steel	0.1
Metal stamping	0.5
Wire and wire products	0.1
Hardware and cutlery	0.1
Other metal fabrication	0.6
Machinery and equipment	
Industrial machinery and equipment	2.4
Commercial, office, and store equipment	2.1
Aircraft and aircraft parts	0.2
Motor vehicles	0.9
Shipbuilding	1.3
Other transportation equipment	0.1
Small electrical appliances	0.2
Large electrical appliances	0.1
Communication equipment	1.7
Electrical industrial equipment	1.8
Other electrical equipment	0.1
Petroleum refineries	0.1
Industrial and other chemical products	0.1
Scientific equipment	0.3
Miscellaneous manufacturing	0.1
All sectors	**2.6**

Notes: The tariff equivalents were constructed for the most part on the basis of price comparisons. The calculations include all sectors for which positive (i.e., non-zero) protection from quantitative restrictions were reported. Details for selected agricultural and food products are given in tables D5 to D10 of the source cited below.
Source: Adapted from Moroz and Brown (1987, table D1).

TABLE 4.12. Canada: Estimates of Tariff Equivalents of Discriminatory Government Procurement (Federal Non-defense and Provincial Purchases) and Import Price Elasticities for Selected Sectors, 1981 (Tariff Equivalents in Percent)

Sector	Tariff Equivalent	Import Price Elasticities
Other non-metal mines	10.4	1.00
Other knitting	3.2	1.01
Printing	1.7	1.69
Boiler and plate	1.2	1.29
Metal stamping	1.4	1.00
Industrial machinery and equipment	4.4	1.00
Commercial, office, and store equipment	4.8	1.00
Shipbuilding	1.5	1.00
Communication equipment	3.0	1.67
Electrical industrial equipment	3.2	1.67
Petroleum refineries	1.1	2.07
Other petroleum products	1.3	2.07
Pharmaceuticals	2.7	3.82
Scientific equipment	10.6	1.00

Notes: Sectors included for which tariff equivalents exceeded one percent. Calculations were based on the "elasticity" approach as detailed in the source cited below.
Source: Adapted from Moroz and Brown (1987, tables D1 and D2).

Antidumping Measures

Information on the share of Canadian imports affected by antidumping (AD) measures for 1988–93 is provided in table 4.13. In calculating these shares, it is assumed that the ratio of "dumped" imports to domestic shipments for a year prior to an AD finding would remain unchanged. The largest shares of imports subject to AD measures were: leather (9.4%); textiles (4.6%); and primary metal products (3.1%). The percentage of total Canadian imports affected by AD measures averaged 0.6% over the period. A breakdown of Canadian AD measures by country/region of origin is noted in table 4.14 for 1988–93. The United States accounted for 33.3% of all AD measures, while the percentages for the Pacific Rim, Japan, and the European Union-12 were 24.8%, 12.9%, and 12.0, respectively. Also noted in table 4.14 is that a relatively small percentage of Canadian imports were affected by AD measures for the countries/regions listed, the largest being 1.8% for the Pacific Rim. The foregoing calculations are interesting in helping to identify the products and countries/regions most subject to Canadian AD measures. But, in themselves, they do not provide any information about the price and quantity effects entailed by the use of AD measures.

TABLE 4.13. Canada: Imports Affected by Anti-Dumping Measures, by Product, 1988-1993 (Percent)

Product	Share of Product Imports
Leather	9.4
Textiles	4.6
Primary metals	3.1
Printing and publishing	1.6
Beverages	1.3
Agricultural products	1.2
Machinery	0.6
Electrical products	0.4
Other manufacturing	0.6
Non-metallic products	0.4
Fabricated metals	0.3
Paper and allied products	0.2
Chemicals	0.0
Rubber products	0.0
All products	**0.6**

Notes: Results by year for 1988-1993 for leather, textiles, and primary metals are reported in the source cited below.

Source: Adapted from Chapman and Lee (1995, p. 6).

TABLE 4.14. Canada: Imports Affected by Antidumping (AD) Measures by Country/Region of Origin, 1988-1993 (Percent)

Country/Region	AD Measures Percent Distribution of Imports Affected by Trading Partner	Share of Total Canadian Imports
United States	33.3	0.3
Pacific Rim	24.8	1.8
Japan	12.9	1.0
European Union-12	12.0	0.7
Mexico	0.1	0.1
Other	16.9	1.8
Total	**100.0**	

Source: Adapted from Chapman and Lee (1995, pp. 11-12).

Germany

Glismann (1996) has provided calculations of the tariff equivalents of quantitative restrictions against Germany's imports of footwear, toys, tableware, and textiles/clothing from the People's Republic of China (PRC) for years between 1988 and 1994.[1] He used three alternative methods for measuring these tariff equivalents, as follows.

His method 1 assumes that an NTB imposed on imports from the PRC will divert trade to the country which is the "second best" source of supply. The difference between the import price from the PRC and the second cheapest supplier is taken as the estimate of the tariff equivalent. Import prices are measured as c.i.f. unit values of German imports at the 8-digit level of the Harmonized System classification. Using these unit values and information from trading firms on the quality and prices of particular goods, the second cheapest suppliers taken for reference purposes included Taiwan, India, Pakistan, and India.[2]

Method II is based on the assumption of the "law of one price." That is, it is assumed that there is a uniform price for a good under conditions of free trade in all supplying countries. Further assumptions include: (1) use of 8-digit unit value data to represent identical products in all countries; (2) imposition of comparable import restrictions by all European Community (EC) countries against the same foreign suppliers; (3) the same price-raising effects of trade barriers in all EC countries; and (4) absence of barriers to trade among EC countries. If the same product imported under quota is also produced in Germany and exported by Germany to other EC countries, the tariff equivalent is then measured as the difference between the German export price to other EC countries and the price of the good imported from the PRC subject to quota.

Method III is applied to cases in which a multinational enterprise (MNE) sells the same good in two countries, one of which is presumed to have free trade. If the MNE's price to the other country is higher, the difference between the two prices is taken to be a measure of the tariff equivalent of the NTB in the second country. Thus, for example, Glismann had data from a MNE that sold its products both in Germany as well as in Hong Kong, the United States, and Australia.

The results for methods I and II are summarized in table 4.15.[3] It is evident that the calculations based on method II are in almost all cases considerably higher than those for method I. This may possibly reflect differences in the qualities of the products being compared and the assumption that the German export price is the same as the German domestic price.

Norway

Effective Rates of Assistance

Holmoy and Haegeland (1994) have calculated effective rates of assistance (ERA) for seventeen Norwegian industries for 1989 and 1991, taking into account government budget subsidies, indirect commodity taxes, nominal tariffs and NTBs, and electricity market distortions. They measure the assistance effects in terms of the net-of-tax value added price assuming removal of the policies. NTBs are treated in two ways: (1) penetration costs which measure the costs of entering the Norwegian domestic market, examples being discriminatory government procurement and technical standards; and (2) quantitative restrictions such as import quotas or VERs that limit quantities that can be imported. The tariff equivalents of these NTBs are shown together with the nominal tariff rates for the major commodity groups for 1989 and 1991 in table 4.16. The tariff equivalents of NTBs are highest for agricultural commodities, processed food, beverages and tobacco, and chemicals and mineral products. The nominal tariff rates are generally less than 1%, except for processed food and beverages and tobacco.

Effective rates of assistance (ERAs) are shown for the individual sectors for 1991 in table 4.17. It is evident again that agriculture, food processing, and beverages and tobacco had the highest ERAs. For agriculture, domestic subsidies were particularly important, whereas NTBs were the main form of assistance provided to food processing and beverages and tobacco. NTBs were also important, as already noted, for chemical and mineral products and oil production platforms. It is evident, finally, that trade barriers were detrimental to the fishing-and-breeding-of-fish sector because input costs were higher.

TABLE 4.15. Germany: Estimated Tariff Equivalents of Imports of Footwear, Toys, Tableware, and Textiles/Clothing from the People's Republic of China, 1988-1994 (Percent)

	Footwear		Toys		Tableware		Textile/Clothing	
Year	Method I	Method II	Method I	Method II	Method I	Method II	Method I	Method II
1988	81.0	326.0	33.3	79.0	129.4	310.0	64.8	152.5
1989	24.7	367.5	31.5	78.0	146.8	333.0	111.0	366.5
1990	32.0	249.5	48.0	102.0	190.4	481.0	93.5	255.0
1991	31.0	300.0	52.0	86.5	187.2	560.0	108.0	176.5
1992	15.0	271.0	36.0	100.5	306.0	820.0	29.8	50.5
1993	57.8	407.5	35.5	90.0	372.2	644.5	70.3	55.5
1994	65.5	209.0	42.3	98.5	319.8	642.5	38.5	25.5

Notes: The tariff equivalents for Method I are the arithmetic averages of all 8-digit Harmonized System categories for all countries and, for Method II, the average of the reference countries. Calculations of different averages are also provided in the source cited below. The averages for textiles/clothing refer to: shorts; T-shirts; jerseys; and pullovers.

Source: Glismann (1996, tables 2-5).

TABLE 4.16. Norway: Nominal and NTB Equivalent Tariff Rates by Sector, 1989 and 1991 (Percent)

Sector	Nominal tariff rates 1989	Nominal tariff rates 1991	Type of NTB	NTB Equivalent tariff rates 1989	NTB Equivalent tariff rates 1991
Agricultural commodities	0.16	0.41	Q	69	71
Commodities from forestry	0.08	0.01		-	-
Commodities from fisheries	-	-		-	-
Processed food	2.90	3.02	Q	44	49
Beverages and tobacco	1.62	2.75	P	35	30
Textiles and wearing apparel	0.03	0.03	Q	2	1
Wood and wood products	6.32	0.05		-	-
Chemical and mineral products	0.36	0.45	Q/P	10	8
Commodities from printing and publishing	-	0.01		-	-
Mining and quarrying	0.01	-	-	-	-
Pulp and paper articles	0.01	-		-	-
Industrial chemicals	0.37	0.37	Q	3	3
Petrol	-	-		-	-
Fuel oils	-	-		-	-
Metals	0.05	0.07		-	-
Metal products, machinery and equipment	0.68	0.66	P	2	2
Repair	-	-		-	-
Ships	-	-		-	-
Oil production platforms	0.02	-	P	3	3

Notes: - means nil; Q means quantitative restrictions; and P means penetration costs. For most agricultural commodities, the NTB tariff equivalents are based on OECD calculations of Producer Subsidy Equivalents (PSE); for milk and other dairy products, comparisons of Norwegian and Danish prices were used. For processed food, price levels in Denmark were used to assess the differences between Norwegian and international prices. The estimates for textiles and wearing apparel were drawn from Melchior (1993). Allowance was made for monopolization of the domestic market in the cases of fertilizers (included in industrial chemicals), which had an estimated implicit tariff rate of 80% in 1989 and 81% in 1991 and cement (included in chemicals and mineral products), which had an estimated implicit tariff rate of 16% in 1989 and 1991. Standards were taken into account for beverages and tobacco, with an estimated tariff equivalent of 35% in 1989 and 30% in 1991. Standards were also taken into account for pharmaceutical products (included in chemical and mineral products) and some commodities included in metal products, machinery, and equipment. A tariff equivalent of 3% was estimated for oil production platforms to allow for discriminatory government procurement in 1989 and 1991. Further details on the construction of the NTB ad valorem tariff equivalents are provided in Faehn (1996).

Source: Holmoy and Haegeland (1994, table 2).

TABLE 4.17. Norway: Effective Rates of Assistance (ERAs) of Different Policy Measures, 1991 (Percent)

Sector	Net Sector Subsidies	Commodity Taxes	Trade Policies	Regulated Electricity Prices	Total ERA
Agriculture	72.2	–2.0	33.0	–0.9	102.3
Food processing	3.2	–7.6	87.9	–0.8	84.3
Manufacture of beverages and tobacco	–2.7	–2.9	52.1	–0.5	46.0
Building of ships	27.5	–1.7	–1.6	–0.3	24.0
Manufacture of chemical and mineral products	2.8	–2.7	15.0	0.5	15.6
Manufacture of pulp and paper articles	0.6	–7.2	–1.7	18.9	10.5
Manufacture of oil production platforms etc.	5.3	–2.5	6.3	–0.3	8.8
Mining and quarrying	12.9	–3.9	–1.5	0.7	8.3
Forestry	9.1	–0.8	–1.9	–0.0	6.4
Manufacture of metals	1.3	–14.6	–2.9	22.6	6.3
Fishing and breeding of fish etc	45.4	–9.2	–28.8	–1.5	5.9
Manufacture of industrial chemicals	0.2	–7.0	3.9	8.6	5.8
Manufacture of metal products, machinery and equipment	2.4	–1.9	4.3	–0.0	4.8
Manufacture of textiles and wearing apparel	3.6	–1.4	0.5	–0.4	–2.3
Manufacture of wood and wood products	2.8	–2.1	–1.9	0.4	–0.8
Printing and publishing	3.1	–2.4	–1.7	0.2	–0.9
Petroleum refining	–0.4	–14.9	3.6	1.8	–9.9

Note: The negative signs indicate the percentage reduction in net government assistance for each of the policies individually and in total.
Source: Holmoy and Haegeland (1994, table 5). Copyright © 1994 OECD; reprinted with permission.

Clothing Import Quotas/VERs

Melchior (1993) has analyzed the system of Norwegian quotas for imports of clothing products during the 1980s. He notes (p. 5) that Norway left the Multi-fibre Arrangement (MFA) in 1978 and adopted a global quota system. Norway rejoined the MFA in 1984 and from 1986 onward greatly liberalized the regime for imported clothing. His calculations of the ad valorem equivalents utilized three main sources of information: (1) quota prices in Hong Kong; (2) price changes for restrained suppliers when Norway changed from its own import-quota regime back to the MFA; and (3) changes in market shares following the post-1986 liberalization. Melchior's work is especially noteworthy for its development and implementation of a carefully constructed econometric model of Norway's import regime for clothing.

His main results are summarized in table 4.18 for selected years between 1983 and 1990. What he calls "restrictivity" conforms to what we referred to as "quantity-impact" measures in our earlier discussion. His estimate of "trade diversion" reflects the changes in Norwegian clothing imports from suppliers in Europe who were not constrained by the quota/MFA restrictions. The "quota rent" estimates refer to the calculated ad valorem tariff equivalents of the restrictions applicable in the years shown. These latter estimates are price-comparison measures based on comparison of domestic and import prices or the quota-auction/transfer price method associated with VER-type arrangements. Melchior concluded that Norwegian clothing importers especially benefited from the restrictions, both during the years covered by the import-quota and MFA regimes, by capturing a significant portion of the rents that would be thought to accrue to domestic clothing producers and/or the MFA quota recipients in the exporting countries. The consequence is that the division of the rents between the importing and exporting countries and between firms engaged in distribution and firms engaged in production in the importing country must be taken into account in calculating the effects of the quota/MFA regime on Norwegian economic welfare.

TABLE 4.18. Norway: Quantity- and Price-Impact Measures of Quota Restrictions on Imports of Clothing, 1983-1990 (Percent)

	1983	1985	1986	1990
Restrictivity	30-40	43-52	41-50	10-25
Trade diversion	14-20	22-28	21-26	4-11
Quota rent	29-43	47-65	45-60	8-22

Notes: Restrictivity is how much low-cost imports were reduced because of quotas. Trade diversion is how much demand increased for unrestrained suppliers and domestic production due to quotas. Quota rent is the tariff equivalent of quotas; i.e. the price increase for low-cost imports made possible because of quotas.
Source: Melchior (1993, p. 7).

European Union/United Kingdom

Antidumping Measures

The work of Greenaway et al. (1995) is based on a report submitted to the U.K. Treasury and Department of Trade and Industry. It represents an especially noteworthy effort to provide an econometric, time-series analysis of AD actions implemented by the European Union (EU) for three products: ball bearings; polypropylene film, and semiconductors.[86] Figure 4.1 illustrates how an AD action introduced at a given point in time can be expected to increase the import price and reduce the import volume of the good subject to the action. It may well be, however, that there is a dynamic process of adjustment as domestic and foreign firms alter their behavior in response to the AD action, so that the response of import price and volume would occur gradually rather than discretely. To capture these impacts, Greenaway et al. use an econometric methodology known as *intervention analysis*, which may permit them to identify the timing and impact of an AD action. This involves looking at disturbances or *outliers*, which can be *additive* or *innovational*, depending on whether the impact is immediate or gradual. If there is evidence of the presence of outliers, it is then possible to remove them from the series and to construct an *outlier free* series which presumes the absence of the AD action and which can be used to assess the welfare effects involved.

In the case of ball bearings, the EU implemented a series of AD actions beginning in the early 1980s. To investigate the impacts of these actions, Greenaway et al. used data for the United Kingdom. They found that the average provisional AD duty (ADD) was 22% on ball bearing imports in the period from March to June 1984, and the average definitive ADD was 20% thereafter for the foreign producers who were targeted by the AD actions.[87] An AD action was taken for polypropylene film imported from Japan in mid-1981. Greenaway et al. found evidence of an increase of about 50% in U.K. prices and lower import volumes.[88] This case was complicated, however, by the existence of a cartel arrangement in the EU, which made it difficult to distinguish the impacts of the AD action from the responses of the European producers.[89] An AD action involving EU semiconductor imports from Japan was taken in February 1987. Because of insufficient time series data and the rapid technological change occurring with semiconductors, it was not possible to estimate the price and quantity impacts involved in this case.

The work by Greenaway et al. is an example of an NTB-specific method of measurement that can be used to analyze the price and quantity impacts of the introduction of an NTB. But there are some problems involved. First, in order to implement this method, it is necessary to have sufficient time-series data for reasonably homogeneous products. Second, some difficulty of interpretation may arise since the procedure cannot distinguish AD shocks from other exogenous changes that may occur. This makes it imperative, as Greenaway et al. note, to take knowledge of market conditions and institutional considerations into account so as to minimize the drawing of spurious inferences from the data analysis.

As existing tariffs and NTBs are to be further reduced and/or phased out in the course of implementing the Uruguay Round negotiations, administered protection in the form of AD and CVD actions will most likely become increasingly important. The intervention methodology utilized by Greenaway et al. thus deserves further attention.

United States

We have already indicated in tables 3.4 and 3.6 the estimates of NTB ad valorem equivalents for 1991 and 1993 that have been calculated by the USITC and the methods used for particular sectors. These methods included: (1) price comparisons for seven agricultural sectors, motor vehicles, and maritime transportation; (2) quota-transfer prices for twenty-two categories of textiles and apparel; and (3) cost-push for sugar-containing products. According to the USITC (1995, p. 2-2), there were another twelve sectors that had relatively high tariffs, but were not subject to import-quota restrictions.[90] Linkins and Arce (1994) discuss the different methods noted for measuring U.S. NTBs. They also review the calculations of NTB ad valorem equivalents for Canada

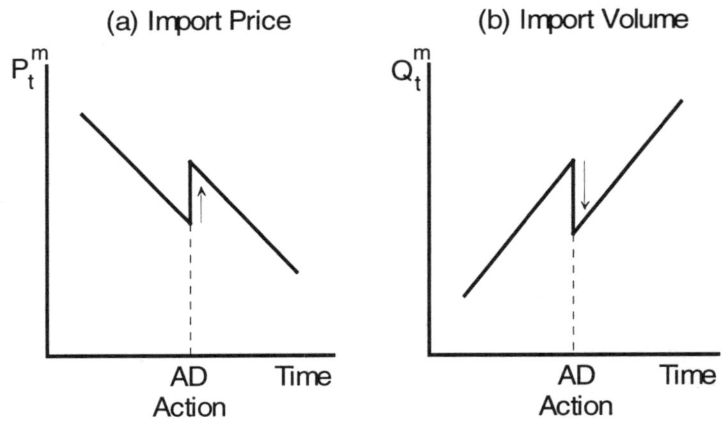

Figure 4.1
Effects of an Antidumping (AD) Action
on Import Price and Volume

Source: Greenaway et al. (1995, p. 49). Copyright © 1995 OECD; reprinted with permission.

that we have presented in table 4.11, in particular based on the work by Moroz and Brown (1987) and Lester and Morehen (1988). Linkins and Arce further note that, as is the case in the United States, most Canadian NTBs were concentrated in the agricultural sector and in textiles and clothing.

Conclusion

The studies summarized here have covered a rich array of methodologies for investigating NTBs. These range from inventories of the trade covered by certain NTBs (Canadian AD measures), to sophisticated econometric time series analysis of trade prices and quantities (United Kingdom AD actions against ball bearings and polypropylene film). Unfortunately, the former do not provide useful quantitative information about the size or restrictiveness of NTBs, while the latter may not be generally applicable. The studies that seem to provide the greatest promise for future work are those that have sought to infer the sizes of known NTBs directly from observations of prices and/or quantities of trade.

The methodologies that appear to have been most successful have varied across industries and types of NTB, but most have involved some sort of price comparison to infer the tariff equivalent of the NTB. These have been provided in the case of Australia, covering quantitative restrictions and several other NTBs in agriculture and general manufacturing; Canada, quantitative restrictions in all sectors; Germany, quantitative restrictions against selected imports from the People's Republic of China; Norway, a variety of NTBs and sectors (some of which have used other methods); and the United States, quantitative restrictions and VERs on several agricultural and industrial products. In addition, quota premia—auction or transfer prices—have been used to measure tariff equivalents of quotas on textile products in Australia, Norway, and the United States. Finally an elasticity approach, inferring tariff equivalents from trade shares and import demand elasticities, has been reported for government procurement restrictions in Canada

Several studies have used these measures of tariff equivalents in turn to construct various measures of the effects of NTBs across industries. These include most obviously the effective rate of assistance calculations for Australia and Norway, but they also include calculation of assistance to "materials" and certain "cost-push" measures of the effects of NTBs on inputs. These measures are valuable in what they disclose about a country's structure of protection, similar to but more comprehensive than effective rates of protection, but they are not the most useful form in which to present data on the sizes of NTBs for other uses. Because these measures already incorporate some information on the input-output linkages within an economy, they are not appropriate for use as inputs to further quantitative analysis such as in an applied general equilibrium model. Therefore the most useful aspects of such studies, for such purposes, are the intermediate results, in which they report, say, nominal rates of assistance.

Therefore, we conclude from this survey that the most useful direction for future investigation of NTBs across industries and countries should be to aim for a comprehensive set of tariff-equivalent measures of protection (nominal, not effective) derived from the most detailed industry-specific information that can be obtained and from various different measurement techniques appropriate to the type of NTB and its method of administration. For many NTBs, this will involve some sort of price comparison, although quota premia, where available, are usually to be preferred. For a few NTBs, such as government procurement, it will be necessary to use other techniques, such as variations of the elasticity approach.

To assist in such investigations, we have constructed in appendix 3 a list of types of NTBs and the circumstances that may accompany them, and we provide explicit formulas for the measurement of tariff equivalents wherever possible. The intent is that this should serve as a kind of handbook for the empirical quantification of NTBs. A guide to the use of this handbook is provided in our concluding chapter that follows.

CHAPTER 5

Guideline Principles and Recommended Procedures for Measuring NTBs

Having discussed at length the various methods of measuring NTBs and some of the main features and results of selected OECD country studies, we present in this concluding chapter a set of guideline principles and recommended procedures for measuring NTBs.

Guideline Principles

1. A measure of an NTB may be viewed as "equivalent" to a certain tariff in the sense that it will lead to the same value as the tariff for some economic indicator. Except in very special circumstances, a measure that is equivalent for one indicator will not be equivalent for others. Potential indicators could include: the quantity (or value) of trade, the domestic price of the imported good, the quantity of domestic production, the level of assistance to domestic producers, etc. Which of these indicators is best depends on the purpose for which the measures will be used. Since calculations of tariff equivalents serve a wide variety of purposes, our view is that they should be based on an indicator that incorporates as few as possible assumptions about economic behavior. *We therefore recommend that measures of NTBs be constructed to reflect equivalence to tariffs in terms of their effects on the domestic prices of the traded goods.*
2. For many purposes input-output relationships are critical for understanding the full effects of a structure of protection. However, we do not recommend that these be incorporated at all into the measures of the tariff equivalents of NTBs. *Thus the effects on domestic prices that are used to define tariff equivalence should be only direct effects,* and they should not, for example, take account of the effect of a barrier in one industry on price in another that uses the first as an input. To include such effects would leave the meanings of individual *TE's* unclear (since they would include effects from other industries' barriers). By reporting *TE's* reflecting only direct effects on domestic prices, the results will be well-suited to performing additional analysis of this sort, such as calculating effective rates of protection or assistance, incorporation into an AGE model, or calculation of the Anderson-Neary Trade Restrictiveness Index.

3. *There is no single method that can be relied upon to measure the sizes of NTBs that may be present in all sectors of the economy.* Methods do exist that seem to have the potential to accomplish that, but in practice these general methods are too unreliable to be used uncritically. Rather, *the "general" methods may be useful for non-general purposes, where NTBs of particular kinds that are amenable to measurement by these methods are known to exist.*
4. *There is no substitute for NTB-specific expertise.* The reliability of any measures of NTBs that may be constructed for particular sectors is limited by the knowledge of the intricacies of those sectors that has been brought to bear upon the measures. The OECD pilot studies include numerous instances in which measurements of NTBs have been influenced in essential ways by such specialized knowledge of products whose trade is being influenced by policy, of the institutional characteristics of both suppliers and demanders, and of the many specialized as well as general government policies that impact on the industries concerned.
5. *Greatest reliance should be placed, where possible, on measures that derive their information from market outcomes in preference to measures that seek to construct estimates of market outcomes from quantitative data.* Thus, for example, observed prices of quota rights where they can be obtained from competitive auctions or from secondary markets are to be preferred to more indirect methods of inferring the tariff equivalent of a quota, such as by comparison of prices in different markets (where the relationship between those markets has to be assumed and/or constructed). Both of these methods should be preferred to estimates of tariff equivalents based upon an elasticity approach starting with a quantity of demand that is assumed to be constrained.
6. Notwithstanding the previous point, however, *in practice there are many NTBs for which high-quality measures are simply not available.* An elasticity estimate of the tariff equivalent of a government procurement regulation, for example, seems to be the best measure that is possible for that particular kind of NTB. In that case it is better to use the only method available, no matter how flawed, than to bias downwards the overall measurement of NTBs by omitting those that are hard to measure.
7. *A scientifically ideal approach to measuring NTBs, given the considerable uncertainty that exists about them, would be to construct approximate confidence intervals—upper and lower bounds—that can be assumed with some degree of confidence to include the actual size of each NTB being measured.* This would serve the desirable purpose of indicating clearly the degree of uncertainty that attaches to the estimates. In practice, however, most users of these estimates will not know what to make of such confidence intervals, and they will either ignore the results entirely or will arbitrarily pick some number inside the interval, most likely its midpoint, as the only estimate to which they will pay attention. Therefore, we recom-

mend that those who measure NTBs themselves be the ones who provide such point estimates, rather than intervals, and that they indicate what the bases of those point estimates are. Their objective should be to provide point estimates that are unbiased in the sense that the true size of each NTB is equally likely to be above the estimate as below it.[1]

8. *Regarding aggregation, we recommend that the estimates of NTBs be done at the most disaggregated levels possible,* since aggregation hides cross-product differences in NTBs that cause distortions. These these most disaggregated estimates should be made available to any users of the results, leaving to them to decide whether and how to aggregate the estimates for their own purposes (since the optimal method of aggregation will depend on the purpose for which the numbers are being used). It will also be necessary, however, to report more aggregated measures of NTBs in order to summarize what has been found. For that purpose we recommend the following:

   Weighted averages should use weights as near as possible to top of the following list. In some cases it may be necessary to aggregate in steps, using domestic import weights at the lowest levels of aggregation and then switching to one of the other weights higher up.

   i. World production
   ii. World trade
   iii. Domestic production
   iv. Domestic imports

   When it is known that an NTB prevails in only a portion of an aggregated category, instead of reporting only a single average TE for that category, the report should always include at least two numbers: the average TE for the covered portion of the category, plus the fraction of the total category that this represents in terms of whatever weights from the above list are being used.[2]

Recommended Procedures for Measuring NTBs

Our recommended procedures for measuring NTBs and the assumptions that apply in particular cases are noted in the outline below. In appendix 3, we present the pertinent notation and algebraic formulas that are applicable in each case.

Steps for Measuring NTBs

I. Identify the presence of NTBs by type and sector.

II. For each NTB-sector pair, determine the availability of the following information, listed in decreasing order of reliability for measuring the size of the NTB.

   A. Market prices for the rights to trade under the NTB

1. Quota-auction prices
2. Quota-transfer prices

B. Comparable data for the imported good and a domestic substitute
1. C.i.f. price of import and ex factory price of substitute
2. Wholesale prices together with additional estimates of relative wholesale distribution costs
3. Retail prices together with additional estimates of relative wholesale plus retail distribution costs

C. Comparable retail or wholesale prices for imported good and for the same good exported to another unprotected market, together with estimates of any differences in transportation costs, tariffs, and distribution costs.

D. Comparable ex-factory prices for the imported good in its country of origin, both for export and for sale to its own domestic market.

E. Comparable quantities of imported and domestic good purchased by someone unconstrained by NTB (e.g., use private-sector demand for comparison in government procurement cases).

III. Identify the NTB and assess the accuracy of the sets of assumptions for which formulas are provided for that NTB in appendix 3. Those assumptions are collected below together with the equation numbers of the formulas from appendix 3.

A. Import Quotas

It is necessary first to determine to whom the quotas are allocated and how. Then pick the appropriate entry from the outline below.

1. If quotas are auctioned
   a. If the auction is plausibly competitive, use formula (I.A.1) for TE^{AUC}.
   b. If auction prices are available for some reference country but not others, the auction prices of the others can be estimated from data on wages and labor productivity there and in the reference country.
   c. If auction is thought to be significantly less than perfectly competitive, use the techniques listed below for quotas that are given away.
2. If quotas are exchanged (transferred) on a plausibly competitive secondary market, use the transfer price in place of the auction price in formula (I.A) for TE^{AUC} above.
3. If quotas are allocated to domestic residents, and if there are enough sellers in the relevant markets to justify assuming perfect

competition, do the following, depending on availability of markets for goods with comparable characteristics or distribution costs:

a. For a good with a perfect domestic substitute, use comparison of c.i.f. price with ex-factory price of domestic substitute in formula (I.C.1) for TE^{SUBST}.

b. If the imported good is a perfect substitute for the domestic good but at a discount reflecting natural disadvantages of imports, use the discounted comparison with the domestic price in formula (I.C.2) for TE^{DISC}.

c. If a good has no perfect domestic substitute but is itself sold by the foreign producers also in one or more other countries with no quota, use comparison of prices at the same stage of distribution (wholesale or retail) across countries in formula (I.C.3) for TE^{EXP}.

d. If a perfect domestic substitute does not exist, but there is an imperfect substitute for which domestic distribution costs are deemed likely to be similar to those of the imported good (or linearly related to those costs), then use comparison of wholesale or retail prices of these goods in formula (I.C.4) for TE^{IMP}.

4. If import quotas are allocated to a small number of domestic residents, so that quota holders have some market power, it is still possible to use the formulas for TE^{SUBST}, TE^{EXP}, and TE^{IMP} so long as producers of the good for export are perfectly competitive.

5. If import quotas are allocated to foreigners, then export prices include some quota rents, and formulas for TE^{SUBST} and TE^{IMP}, which compare to the c.i.f. price, cannot be used.

   a. So long as the quotas are not allocated to the foreign producers themselves, and if these producers are competitive, then formula (I.C.3) for TE^{EXP} can still be applied.

   b. If quotas are allocated to foreign producers, then formula (I.C.3) for TE^{EXP} can be applied if these foreign producers also sell the same product in another NTB-free export market and if

      (1) Producers would have been competitive without the NTB, or

(2) Producers are not perfectly competitive, but can be assumed to earn the same monopoly rents per unit in both markets without the quota.

c. If it is certain that all rents from the quota are confined to the foreign producer, then formula (I.C.3) for TE^{EXP} may be adapted to compare between c.i.f. prices, f.o.b. prices, or even ex factory prices. The formula in this last case will be the same as formula (I.E.3) for TE^{OWN}.

d. If quotas are allocated to foreign producers who do not export to a third country market, but who do sell the same product with the same marginal cost of production in their own domestic market, and if market power can be assumed the same in both markets absent the quota, then compare ex-factory prices to the two markets using formula (I.E.3) for TE^{OWN}.

If ex-factory prices are not available, or if quota rents are thought to accrue partly at later stages of distribution, then comparison of own-country and import prices at later stages may be attempted using formula (I.E.3*) for TE-OWN^*. However, these comparisons require rather detailed data on shipping, transportation, and distribution costs plus tariffs.

6. If the rents due to a quota are thought to be shared by resident individuals or firms in both the exporting country and the importing country, then formula (I.C.3) for TE^{EXP}—comparing retail or wholesale prices in the domestic market with another quota-free export market and taking account of differences in distribution costs and tariffs—can still be used, since it includes rents in both countries.

7. If there are no imports at all under a quota, as in the case of an embargo, then the above formulas may still be applied if surveys of market participants can determine at what prices imports would be available if there were no restriction. If that is not possible, then estimates of these prices may be constructed from prices to other export markets and estimates of transportation costs, using formula (I.G) for TE^{EMBARG}.

8. Tariff-Quotas: A tariff-quota, which permits imports above quota at a higher tariff rate than applies to within-quota imports, can be examined by combining any of the above formulas for a simple quota with the out-of-quota tariff rate, using formula (I.H) for $TE^{T\text{-}Q}$.

B. Variable Levies

1. If the export market is reasonably competitive, then use the revenues from the levy relative to the value of trade to measure its tariff equivalent in formula (II.A) for TE^{VAR1}.
2. If foreign exporters are imperfectly competitive, then use comparisons of f.o.b. prices into the import market with f.o.b. prices into other export markets, together with the levy revenues, to infer the size of the levy using formula (II.B) for TE^{VAR2}.
3. Alternatively, if f.o.b. prices are difficult to observe, one can compare prices mandated by the variable levy with inside border prices in other markets using formula (II.C) for TE^{VAR3}.

C. Voluntary Export Restraints

Tariff equivalents are given by the same formulas listed above for quotas that are allocated to foreigners.

D. Government Procurement Regulations

1. If the regulation takes the form of an explicit preference (buy domestic goods unless imports are at least x% cheaper), then use formula (IV.A) for TE^{GOV1}.
2. If the regulation is only implicit, then use formula (IV.B) for TE^{GOV2}.

E. Countervailing Duties

Countervailing duties (CVDs) should be measured directly from the sizes of the duties as they are levied, based on the records of the outcomes of CVD cases.

F. Anti-Dumping Duties

1. All duties that are currently being levied as a result of past and present AD cases should be recorded, converted if necessary to ad valorem terms, and included in any general quantification of NTBs. If these duties have already been included along with other tariffs, then they must not be double-counted, but it is desirable to separate them from other tariffs because they have somewhat different effects.
2. All AD cases should be examined for this purpose, not just those that have led to a positive determination and the levying of a duty. All cases that were settled prior to a final determination should also be included, and the nature of any settlement should be quantified and included in any measure of anti-dumping as an NTB. Such settlements can take many forms, and their quantification will seldom be straightforward. The following are two examples that could be used as guides to actual cases:

a. If the settlement takes the form of a "price undertaking," in which the foreign exporter agrees to keep price at some higher level, a comparison of the promised price with recent past prices will yield a percentage difference that can be taken as the TE of the undertaking.

b. If the settlement takes the form of a "quantity undertaking" or a "market share undertaking," in which the foreign exporter agrees in some fashion to limit sales in the domestic market, this can be quantified with an elasticity approach, using formula (VI.B.2) for TE^{SET}.

3. While there is no general way of inferring the trade-reducing effects of a whole complex of AD laws in many countries, it is possible that if a particular country/sector is suspected of being especially prone to AD actions, the resulting discouraging effect on trade may be picked up by using the comparison of export prices in the formula for TE^{EXP} in (I.C.3).

G. Domestic Content Requirements

Domestic content requirements can take many forms, and it is therefore essential that they be examined closely to determine exactly how they are constructed and what effects they are likely to have.

1. A content requirement typically says that some percentage of a good's content must be sourced domestically in return for a specified benefit. If a firm opts not to satisfy the requirement, or if it opts to include more than the required percentage of domestic content, then the requirement has had no effect and its tariff equivalent is zero.
2. If a content requirement is satisfied and binding, then its tariff equivalent may be calculated from formula (VII.B) for TE^{CON1}.
3. If the benefit from satisfying a content requirement is that inputs may be imported free of duty, then one can use formula (VII.C) for TE^{CON2}.

H. Customs Valuation Procedures

1. If valuation procedures are well defined, but do not accord with the standard of valuing at the f.o.b. free-market price, then the preferred method of dealing with them is not to calculate any NTB at all, but rather to recalculate the true ad valorem tariff rates relative to f.o.b. free-market prices.
2. If for some reason the recalculation of tariff rates is not possible, then the tariff equivalent of customs valuation procedures can be calculated using formula (VIII.B) for TE^{VAL}.

3. If uncertainty about customs valuation is thought to further restrict imports, then the tariff equivalent of that uncertainty may be evaluated using a price comparison. If the producing firm sells the product also in another export market that is not subject to this uncertainty or other NTBs, or if it sells the product in its own domestic market, then the formulas (I.C.2) for TE^{EXP} or (I.E.3) for TE^{OWN} can be used.

I. Technical Barriers to Trade

If regulatory and/or certification mechanisms are designed in a way that puts imports at a disadvantage relative to domestic goods, this is one of the hardest NTBs imaginable to quantify. Our only general suggestion, aside from trying to extract credible assessments of their costs from affected industries as indicated below, is again to use formulas (I.C.2) for TE^{EXP} or (I.E.3) for TE^{OWN} that are based on comparisons with other export markets or with the own domestic market of the exporter.

1. If imports and domestic goods are subject to different standards, the costs of satisfying which are known, then the tariff equivalent can be calculated from formula (IX.A) for TE^{STAND1}.
2. If imports and domestic goods are subject to a single standard that is enforced differently for imports than for domestic goods, then formula (IX.B) for TE^{STAND2} can be used in terms of the fractions of units of the good that satisfy the standard.
3. If certification requirements are different for domestic and imported goods, then the costs of certification can be used like the costs of the standards themselves, in formula (IX.A) for TE^{STAND1}.

J. Domestic Subsidies

Domestic subsidies cannot be quantified in terms of tariff equivalents, since there do not exist tariffs that would have the same effects on prices as a subsidy. Nor can their effects on quantities of trade be easily ascertained, since these depend on the context of the markets in which they are applied. We therefore recommend instead that domestic subsidies be quantified in terms of their Output Subsidy Equivalents, OSE, and we provide several formulas for this measure in particular circumstances.

1. Subsidies that are paid directly for output, or that are paid for inputs that vary with output, can be quantified using formula (X.A) for OSE^{OUT}.
2. Subsidies that are paid on an ongoing basis over time but that are not related to output may nonetheless have a positive OSE if they prevent a firm from shutting down. Formula (X.B) permits cal-

culation of one such measure, OSE^{IND1}, in terms of the amount of the subsidy and a comparison of prices and long-run average costs.

3. If a subsidy independent of output is only temporary, then a similar comparison to short-run variable costs yields formula (X.C) for OSE^{IND1}.
4. If a subsidy is paid only once, it can still be related to output as in the case of a capital subsidy. Formula (X.D) uses the interest rate to translate the one-time payment into an equivalent flow over time in OSE^{OUT0}. A one time subsidy that is not related to output, however, has no output effect at all, and its OSE is zero.

IV. Select formula for measuring the TE of the NTB from those that might apply. If more than one are feasible in terms of available data, select on the basis of the accuracy of the assumptions needed for each formula, attempting at the same time to identify the direction of any bias that use of the particular formula might imply. Apply the chosen formula to calculate the TE of the NTB.

Notes

Notes to Chapter 2

1. For somewhat different typologies of NTBs, see Greenaway et al. (1995, pp. 6-11) and Laird (1996, esp. appendix II). The UN Conference on Trade and Development (UNCTAD) coding system of trade control measures is reproduced in Laird (1996, appendix I) and in OECD (1996). The UNCTAD coding system, which refers only to import-related measures, is most commonly used in constructing measures of NTB frequencies and import/production-weighted coverage ratios. These are discussed in chapter 3.

2. Incidentally, as already mentioned, the term NTB commonly encompasses trade-expanding policies such as subsidies in addition to trade-restricting policies. While in our general discussion we will treat all NTBs as trade-restricting, it should be understood that some NTBs may be negative and serve to stimulate trade.

3. If there is also a tariff, this demand curve could be drawn taking it into account, and the analysis would capture the additional effects of the NTB. However, for ease of exposition we will refer to this as the free trade demand curve.

4. The logarithmic representation means that the elasticity (η) will be constant for any given straight line demand curve. This can be strictly correct, of course, only in the case of imperfect substitutes. Note also, depending on the currency used to measure the price, p, the position of either the supply curve or the demand curve will depend on the exchange rate. In what follows, we abstract from changes in the exchange rate, although we will take account of exchange rates in the measurement formulas of appendix 3.

5. As usual with supply and demand analysis of market interventions (such as taxes), equivalent results can be obtained by altering either the supply curve or the demand curve, depending on whose price is to be read from their intersection. Here we let that be the exporters' price, so that it is the demand curve that shifts or changes shape.

6. The rise in slope (and hence the fall in elasticity) in this case occurs because we measure prices in logarithms. Graphed instead with the price level (received by foreign exporters) on the axis, the demand curve would shift down by the constant amount of the extra cost, thus becoming less elastic at every quantity.

7. The shadow price is relevant in other cases such as a government procurement restriction that requires government agencies to purchase domestically produced goods unless their price exceeds that of imports by more than a fixed percentage. In this case, if the government has the same elasticity of demand as the private sector, the (logarithmic) demand curve is shifted down, without a change in slope, by a fraction of that percentage, the fraction being the government's initial shares of imports. We will have more to say about procurement restrictions in chapter 3.

8. For example, if the imports were provided by a foreign monopolist, then supply curve SS would not exist, and the initial quantity, q_0, would have been found from the intersection of a marginal cost curve (evidently one lower than SS) with the marginal revenue curve corresponding to DD. A new marginal revenue curve corresponding to D′D′ would determine, together with marginal cost, the quantity with the NTB.

9. One could also normalize on quantity, asking by how much price would have to fall to maintain q_0 in the presence of the NTB. This becomes infeasible, however, if the NTB places an upper limit on q that is below q_0.

10. As noted earlier, an ad valorem tariff shifts the logarithmic demand curve down by the percent of the tariff without changing its slope. Since the NTB in general changes the slope of the demand curve, there is no single tariff that can be regarded as in all respects equivalent to it. A tariff of $p_1' - p_1$ would yield the same outcome as the NTB given the supply curve SS, and so might be considered the most appropriate candidate for a tariff equivalent. But then, again, the tariff equivalent would include information about supply as well as the NTB itself. The distance $p_2 - p_0$ might therefore be regarded as a somewhat purer form of tariff equivalent, one that is normalized so as to reflect only the nature of the NTB. We will have more to say about the concept of tariff equivalents in chapter 3.

11. Even for a tariff, of course, the single number representing its *ad valorem* or specific value is not sufficient to describe its full effects on domestic prices and quantities, which depend also on whether supply is perfectly competitive and, if so, on the elasticity of supply.

12. Note from figure 2.1 that the price and quantity effects of an NTB are directly related to each other through the elasticity of demand for imports. Thus if elasticities are known, only one of these two characteristics needs to be measured independently.

13. If the good in question is an intermediate input, then the demand curve does not directly yield consumer surplus. However, it can be argued that the same geometric method captures the welfare effect working through the costs and prices of final goods in the production of which the import is used. See Wisecarver (1974).

14. For a treatment of welfare costs, see Richard Baldwin (1994, esp. pp. 26-29). Baldwin distinguishes between rent-creating barriers and cost-creating barriers. In the former case, the price gap created by the barriers is captured by whomever is granted the import licenses. In the latter case, the barriers raise the real cost of importing the goods. Rent-creating barriers include, for example, import quotas and voluntary export restraints. Cost-creating barriers include government procurement regulations, domestic content requirements, antidumping and countervailing duties, customs valuation procedures, and technical barriers that may be designed at least in part to protect domestic firms and service providers against foreign competition.

15. These resource costs reduce welfare just as much as do the "welfare" costs in item 6. The welfare costs are given that name only because they have been the traditional focus of welfare economics.

16. There may also be prior lobbying costs incurred in trying to get the authorities to impose the NTBs.

Notes to Chapter 3

17. For a description of the UNCTAD Database, see OECD (1996, Annex 1).

18. It is also possible to conduct special surveys of how trading firms perceive or experience NTBs, or the number of complaints that firms may file with government agencies. See U.S. Tariff Commission (1974) for survey evidence on the experience and complaints that U.S. trading firms reported about particular NTBs. Frequency distributions were constructed for all NTBs covered in the survey as well as broken down for each type of NTB, country, and commodity group.

19. In addition to these "Quad" countries, results for other OECD countries--former EFTA members (Austria, Finland, and Sweden), EFTA members (Iceland, Norway, and Switzerland), Australia, New Zealand, Mexico, Turkey, and Korea—are presented in OECD (1996).

20. "Core" NTBs are those NTBs normally intended to modify or restrict international trade. "Hard core NTBs" refer to QRs and PCMs.

21. See Greenaway et al. (1995, pp. 11-19) for an analysis of European Union NTBs for 1992 by type of NTB and broken down according to the 2-digit SITC classification. Studies of NTB frequencies and trade coverage for earlier years for the OECD and other countries include Laird and Yeats (1990) and Laird and Vossenar (1991).

22. See OECD (1996) for some other calculations of NTBs, including the extent to which NTBs are escalated according to the degree of processing, substitution or complementarity rela-

tions between sectoral tariffs and NTBs, and changes from 1988 to 1993 in the use of NTBs relative to tariffs.

23. See Leamer (1990a,b) for efforts to use the NTB coverage data to assess the impact of NTBs on trade flows in 1983 for the major industrialized and developing countries.

24. The discussion here ignores within country distribution and transport costs. These complications, among others, are taken into account in the formulas of appendix 3.

25. For this reason, Sazanami, Urata, and Kawai (1995), in their study of the cost of protection for Japan, have used "unit values" of imported and domestic goods as proxies for prices. Using unit values is in our view problematic because of obvious difficulties in matching imported and domestic goods and especially controlling for quality differences between these goods. The difficulties would appear to be most serious for manufactured goods in which domestic and imported varieties are imperfect substitutes.

26. Even with perfect substitutes, however, this measure also includes any differences in domestic distribution costs, which we abstract from here. See appendix 3.

27. Again, formulas can be corrected for differences in transport costs, if these are known, using the formulas in appendix 3.

28. For some earlier results, see Baldwin (1975, p. 99), who presented some data on implicit protection on selected commodities in the Philippines for December 1951, using (c.i.f.) import prices and retail prices. He also presented (p. 102) data on U.S. and Philippine wholesale prices for a variety of goods for selected years between 1949 and 1965, and with an adjustment for transport costs, he interpreted the price differences as indicative of Philippine restrictions affecting imports. Bhagwati and Srinivasan (1975, pp. 179-81) provide calculations of implicit tariff rates for India covering 69 products for the years 1963-65 and 1968-69. In some later work, Baldwin (1989, p. 11) noted that price data for 1985 were compiled in Eurostat (1988) for household consumption items and equipment goods for 215 basic headings that covered around 3,000 products. These price data were in turn used by the Commission of the European Communities (1988) to calculate tariff equivalents of NTBs in order to assess the economic effects of the 1992 removal of these barriers. Laird and Yeats (1990, chapter 5) contains a literature survey of a variety of studies in which efforts have been made to calculate ad valorem equivalents by product category and country/region based on differences between domestic and foreign prices for agricultural products, textiles and clothing, steel products, and other manufactured goods.

29. Price-gap measures can also be used to measure the tariff equivalents of quotas on imported inputs for "downstream" and "upstream" sectors. This is referred to as the *cost-push method* in Moroz and Brown (1987) and USITC (1995, p. 7-6). Thus, suppose we have a price-gap estimate for an upstream sector. In this case, we could calculate the tariff equivalent for the downstream sector based on its cost share of production represented by the upstream input. This is the method used for sugar-containing products for the United States for 1991 and 1993. It presumes that the upstream tariff equivalent is calculated accurately and that there is perfect competition in the downstream sector.

30. For some earlier work, see Roningen and Yeats (1976), who compiled price statistics for 1973 covering 90 products in 15 advanced industrialized countries. They assumed the "world" price to be the lowest observed price for a given product specification. Netting out domestic taxes, nominal tariffs and variable levies, and transportation costs in and between countries, they calculated "NTB residuals" for the major product groupings.

31. Linkins and Arce (1994, pp. 4-5) indicate that the extent of coverage and the degree to which MFA quotas were utilized in 1991 varied notably from country to country. This suggests that quota-constrained suppliers may be hesitant to make export commitments, which, if true, can lead to under-utilization of quotas. This does not mean that the quota has no effect, however.

32. For details, see USITC (1995, pp. 7-7 and 7-8).

33. This is evident in figure 2.1 as long as the tariff equivalent is measured using the observable prices, p_1' and p_1.

34. We should mention that, in focusing attention on the quantity effects of an NTB, Jager and Lanjouw (1977) nonetheless looked first at prices. That is, they estimated the tariff equivalent of NTBs in a particular industry, Dutch newsprint, for a number of years in the manner already described. Then they combined the tariff equivalent with separately estimated supply and demand

elasticities to derive the implicit quantity effects. This enabled them to illustrate graphically how the relationship between the price and quantity effects of the NTB varied over time, but it does not provide a really distinct quantity-oriented methodology. See also Hufbauer and Elliott (1994), who base their calculation of the costs of protection for 21 U.S. sectors in 1990 on "guesstimates" of demand and supply elasticities and cross-elasticities in determining how trade would respond if existing NTBs were removed.

35. When confronting actual situations, some allowance may have to be made as well for disequilibrium situations and international capital flows.

36. See Deardorff (1998) for a theoretical analysis of the underpinnings of the gravity model.

37. In addition to the points below, quantity measures may be sensitive to disequilibrium exchange rates. This is the case also for price measures. But, since quantities adjust relatively slowly, this should be less of a problem as compared to price measures.

38. This is not to say that bad models of NTBs always somehow overstate their effects. The point here is only that if we infer NTBs from the difference between actual trade flows and those predicted by some model, as this methodology does, then the further the model strays from reality the larger will these differences be, even if there are no NTBs in fact. Of course, a bad model could coincidentally predict exactly the trade flows that NTBs happen to give rise to, but that seems very unlikely.

39. See Saxonhouse and Stern (1989) for an econometric analysis of this kind in an effort to determine whether Japan's trade performance appears unusual in comparison to other countries, in particular the United States and Canada. While the results provide some suggestions about unusual features of each nation's trade performance at the sectoral level, it is not possible to infer unambiguously what the precise sectoral impact is of NTBs.

40. We should also mention the effects of rent seeking which were investigated in the pioneering work of Krueger (1974), who focused attention on the possible costs in the form of wasted resources that might be incurred in competing for the rents arising from import licensing. Krueger's work has been important in changing the way we think about the costs of trade barriers, and it has led to similar theoretical analysis for trade barriers other than quotas, as in Bhagwati and Srinivasan (1980). However, there has been surprisingly little further empirical work on the subject apart from occasional calculations of the rents that are implicit in various NTBs. Hardly any effort seems to have been made to measure directly the rent seeking activities themselves. For one such effort, see Jackson (1984). See also Tarr (1994).

41. See Saxonhouse (1977) for some methodological considerations that are relevant in these circumstances.

42. As mentioned above, Linkins and Arce (1994) have noted in connection with the MFA that quota utilization may vary by country and time period and that less than full utilization of quotas may reflect market uncertainties that constrain exporters. Thus, in measuring the quota-auction price tariff equivalents for MFA quotas in the United States, the USITC (1995) used utilization rates of 80% and 90%. We are not entirely clear, however, as to what role these utilization rates played in their analysis. If the auction price of a quota in a particular market is positive, then the tariff equivalent of the quota is at least that large regardless of the rate of utilization. However, USITC (1995) had auction prices only for imports from Hong Kong, and they used those data to infer tariff equivalents of quotas from other exporters. It was presumably here that they used the utilization rates.

43. It would be interesting to determine if there is any kind of insurance that firms can use to cover themselves against adverse trade policy actions. In this connection, firms are sometimes required to post bond at the beginning of a possible trade action. The size of this bond is itself an NTB, but presumably it also provides some indication of the perceived likelihood that the trade action will be decided against the firm.

44. The work on European Union antidumping (AD) actions by Greenaway et al. (1995), which will be discussed below, is an effort of this kind.

45. Export quotas are also possible, and their analysis is analogous.

46. Actually, it is quite common to have both a tariff and a quota on a given good, so that a tariff is paid on units of the good that are admitted under the quota. This should be distinguished

from a "tariff-quota", which is a tariff that increases, discretely, at a certain level or levels of quantity imported. We will confine our attention here, however, to a pure quota that is not accompanied in any way by a tariff. Both accompanying tariffs and tariff quotas will be allowed for in appendix 3.

47. If importers are risk averse and unable to diversify or otherwise offset the risk that their price expectations will be incorrect, then the price of a license will be somewhat less than the expected price difference. This means that part of the price difference will not go to the government as revenue, but will compensate traders for their real loss of utility.

48. On the other hand, some of these "distortions" could be desirable. For example, if the domestic market is already oligopolistic and the quota were allocated in proportion to sales, then the incentive to expand sales would offset somewhat the inefficiencies of the oligopoly. Of course the quota itself is likely to reduce competition substantially, so the net effect of the quota is still likely to be adverse.

49. For example, it is intriguing to consider the administratively simple scheme of allocating the quota on a first-come-first-served basis in each calendar year. With competition, this will cause the domestic price of the import to be lower early in the year than later. How the quantity of imports is altered, and the precise time path followed by the price, depend however on the feasibility of storing the good. If it is storable and the quota is not too small, for example, one may find the market undistorted during the first part of the year, with the remainder of the quota being imported all at once at some date during the year, and the price rising smoothly thereafter as though the good were an exhaustible resource.

50. If a perfect substitute is produced domestically, then this is not a problem, since the price of the domestic good will equal $\hat{p}$. But if domestic goods in the industry are imperfect substitutes for imports, then the error of using a price index instead of the price of imports will be exacerbated by this failure of directly allocated intermediate imports to be included in the index.

51. The comparison of domestic prices in the two countries, used in IT^2, is not undermined so severely, since presumably foreign governments would not tax their own markets when they tax exports, but we already noted other doubts about the validity of this measure.

52. See Feenstra (1984) for such an approach to the auto industry.

53. See, for example, Bhagwati and Srinivasan (1975, pp. 160-61) for data on premium rates for import licenses in India covering selected products on a monthly basis during 1966. More recent data are to be found in Industry Commission (1995) and Melchior (1993). As discussed earlier in connection with VERs, licenses for exports are sometimes traded freely and the prices for these licenses may be indicative of the impact of the quota. In particular, information from Hong Kong has been used to calculate the quota rents on textiles and clothing subject to the MFA.

54. Studies of variable levies and related policies include Sampson and Snape (1980) and Sampson and Yeats (1976, 1977). Additional references can be found in Laird and Yeats (1990).

55. Variable levies have been only one part of the European Community's Common Agricultural Policy, which has also involved domestic price supports for certain goods and adjustments of target prices to take intercountry exchange-rate changes into account. As a result of the Uruguay Round, these and other border measures have been converted into equivalent tariffs. For further discussion and details, see especially Hathaway and Ingco (1996).

56. There is no difference in responses to changes abroad. Since both policies lead to the same distorted demand curve, they also cause identical responses to shifts of foreign supply.

57. In fact only the target price, and not the size of the levy collected, is normally publicly available anyway.

58. The latter may differ from both of the former by involving both a more formal institutional structure and a larger number of participating countries.

59. Or, equivalently, that the VER is negotiated with all foreign exporters. The case of a VER implemented by only a subset of exporters is more interesting, as we will note below, but it is also more complicated and is beyond what we can pursue in any detail here.

60. See our earlier discussion of the quota-auction price method.

61. One further complication is left out of the analysis in figure 3, but may be quite important. As noted above, in practice VERs are often negotiated with only a subset of foreign suppliers,

and one of their effects is to stimulate increases in supply from other sources. The most straightforward way of evaluating a VER, by simply comparing the permitted quantity to that which was coming in immediately before the VER was put in place, will considerably overstate the importance of the VER if this effect is neglected. A similar source of bias arises if the VER fails to cover exports of close substitutes even from the same country. Producers are quite adept at changing their product lines to penetrate loopholes in a negotiated restraint.

62. An indication of how complicated this can be, especially for imports of a differentiated product, may be found in Berry et al. (1995) who estimate the effects of the VER on autos imported by the United States from Japan.

63. See Hoekman (1997) for data and analysis for 1983-93 of various aspects of actual procurement by government entities in the major industrialized countries that are subject to the Government Procurement Agreement (GPA). He concludes that the GPA has not accomplished a great deal thus far in opening markets. Since government procurement accounts for a sizable proportion of total expenditures in many countries, there appears to be considerable potential for removing existing barriers in both the major industrialized and developing countries. It should be noted that the GPA was one of the few parts of the Uruguay Round agreements that was not to be applied automatically to all members of the World Trade Organization.

64. Lowinger (1976) has assessed the effects of government procurement restrictions by calculating what government imports would be if the government had the same import propensities as the private sector. This assumption was also used by Moroz and Brown (1987) for Canada, as will be noted below. Another noteworthy study of the discriminatory impacts of government procurement policies is Baldwin and Richardson (1972). For a discussion of the methodology used in these and other studies, see Francois, Nelson, and Palmeter (1997).

65. This is the case in Canada insofar as government nondefense purchases of goods accounted for a small proportion of total purchases. As noted in table 4.12 below, only fourteen of the ninety-two Canadian industries covered had a calculated tariff equivalent in excess of one percent. A similar conclusion was reached by Francois, Nelson, and Palmeter (1997) for the United States, based on 1992 data. They suggested, however, that this conclusion may not carry over to services since government nondefense procurement is relatively sizable in a number of services sectors. See also Deltas and Evenett (1997) for theoretical analysis and simulation results for the effects of government preference policies on firm profits and procurement costs and implications for future liberalization of government procurement practices.

66. The import price elasticities used in calculating the tariff equivalents for Canadian government procurement for fourteen sectors are listed in table 4.12. The elasticity estimates for all ninety-two sectors are given in table D2 of Moroz and Brown (1987). These estimates came from the Canadian Department of Finance.

67. Perhaps the most ambitious efforts to measure subsidies are those described in OECD (1986) for the agricultural sector in the major OECD countries. These include measures of producer and consumer subsidy equivalents. The producer subsidy equivalents (PSEs) are a measure of the payment or subsidy that would be required to compensate producers for the removal of government agricultural assistance programs of various kinds. The consumer subsidy equivalents (CSEs) measure the implicit tax on consumption from agricultural policy measures as well as subsidies to consumption.

68. In this figure the quantities themselves are graphed, rather than their logarithms as were used in the preceding figures. This is necessary, since the excess demand curve takes on both positive and negative values, and incidentally therefore cannot have constant elasticity as was assumed before.

69. A tariff equivalent would exist if equivalence were defined in terms of, say, effect on quantity of trade or assistance to domestic industry. We do not pursue these options here, having decided that for most trade barriers equivalence in terms of effects on domestic prices provides the most useful measure. Subsidies, where they exist, must therefore be handled separately.

70. Subsidies to inputs have additional effects, of course, in addition to their effect on output, since they alter the mix of inputs that are employed. Thus two subsidies with the same OSE may not be equivalent in terms of their effects on things other than output, just as two NTBs with the same tariff equivalents may have different effects on variables other than price.

71. Note that area G cancels out for the firm, being a tariff cost without compliance and a real input cost with compliance. The country as a whole, however, would have retained the tariff revenue. From the country's point of view, compliance causes only the real resource loss of areas G+D.

72. For some empirical evidence on this point, see Messerlin (1988).

73. See Hoekman and Kostecki (1995, esp. pp. 112-20) for a discussion of technical regulations and standards with reference especially to the economic issues involved, GATT/WTO rules and procedures, and the Uruguay Round Agreement on the Application of Sanitary and Phyto–Sanitary Measures.

74. This is the theme of Baldwin's (1982) Graham lecture.

75. A useful introduction to the calculation and interpretation of the TRI is provided in USITC (1995, pp. 7–10 – 7-13).

76. Among the many single-country AGE models in current use, the best known and by far most sophisticated model is the ORANI model of the Australian economy, details of which can be found in Dixon, Parmenter, Sutton, and Vincent (1982) and in the publications and working papers of the IMPACT project which is currently located at Monash University in Melbourne. An AGE model for the United States is maintained by the USITC (1995) and has been used periodically to assess the economic effects of existing U.S. tariffs and NTBs.

77. Applications of these models can be found in the quantitative assessments of the Uruguay Round negotiations reported in Martin and Winters (1996). These assessments include the effects of tariff reductions, tariffication of agricultural protection and domestic production subsidies and other supports, reduction/removal of NTBs, including the MFA, and the potential for liberalization of international trade in services.

Notes to Chapter 4

78. For calculations of price disadvantage for 48 TCF products subject to quota in 1978, see Industry Commission (1994, table D.1). This source also gives the number of observations for each product category. However, because the quota numbers for the product categories were not reported, it is difficult to compare the 1978 estimates with those in table 4.4.

79. As noted in Industry Commission (1995, pp. 50–51), these include: (1) perfect substitution between domestic and foreign goods of the same description; (2) no substitution between nominally different goods; (3) infinite elasticities of export demand and import supply (i.e., the small country assumption); (4) the direction of trade in the absence of assistance can be assessed, with import-parity prices forming the benchmark for import-competing goods and with export-parity prices for export goods; (5) in the absence of assistance, prices of goods, services, and factors represent their opportunity cost to the community (i.e., absence of domestic distortions); and (6) production relationships between inputs (that is, intermediate inputs and primary factors) are unchanged by the structure of assistance.

80. Estimates of bilateral Canada-U.S. NTB tariff equivalents are presented in Lester and Morehen (1988), based on Moroz and Brown (1987).

81. Additional details of tariff equivalents for selected commodities are given in Moroz and Brown (1987, table 11) and Campbell and Cossette (1994, pp. 21, 28, and 36). These calculations are not comparable, however, to those listed in table 4.11 since they come from different sources and apparently have used different prices for comparative purposes. Nonetheless, it is still the case that most of Canada's NTB protection from quantitative restrictions applies to agricultural and food products and clothing.

82. Their calculations relied on data for federal government purchases available from the Canadian input-output table, price elasticities from Canada's Department of Finance, and a breakdown of federal procurement by domestic and foreign sources from Canada's Department of Supply and Services. Provincial purchases were not broken down by source and were assumed to involve the same average propensity to import as federal nondefense procurement.

83. Glismann also discusses the compatibility of NTBs with GATT regulations, the static and dynamic effects of the imposition of trade barriers, and various methods that have been used for measuring the size of NTBs.

84. There may be some difficulty in using c.i.f. unit values especially for textile/clothing imports from these other Asian suppliers insofar as they include some quota rents. Glismann has attempted to make allowance for this by including Portugal, which is not subject to quotas, as another potential source of supply.

85. Illustrative and more detailed calculations of the tariff equivalents for methods I, II, and III are presented in tables 3–5 of the complete version of Glismann's study. See also pp. 160–67 of the complete study for the results of a detailed analysis based on method III. For four types of tableware, as noted in table 5 (p. 90) of the complete study, the average tariff equivalent based on method III was 16.4 percent for 1993.

86. Greenaway et al. also provide estimates of frequency and coverage ratios on EU imports at the 2-digit SITC level of disaggregation for 1992 as well as information relating to AD and CVD measures implemented by the EU from 1981/83–1993. They discuss the theoretical aspects of the construction and interpretation of NTB tariff equivalents, noting in particular that AD measures pose difficult problems of measurement when market structures are imperfectly competitive or policy-induced distortions exist.

87. Using the procedure noted above to construct an outlier free series, it was estimated that the imposition of the ADDs reduced U.K. economic welfare in 1984 by about one-third of the average monthly value of U.K. imports of ball bearings.

88 The welfare loss was estimated to be about 17% of the U.K. average monthly imports of polypropylene film.

89. Further details on the polypropylene film AD action using intervention analysis are to be found in Lloyd et al. (1998).

90. These sectors included: ball and roller bearings; ceramic wall and floor tile; china tableware; costume jewelry and novelties; footwear; leather products; frozen fruit, juices, and vegetables; products from blast furnaces and steel mills; household audio and video equipment; and industrial chemicals.

Notes to Chapter 5

91. Thus we are suggesting that estimates be taken from the median, rather than the mean, of any distribution. Methods will hardly ever be refined enough to make this distinction, but our point is that if the uncertainty about a particular estimate is very skewed, the median is a more generally useful statistic than the mean, since the latter is unit dependent.

92. The idea here is that what matters most about trade barriers for at least some purposes, such as economic efficiency, is differences in protection, not just levels. Reporting just the average for a category—which will in any case still be available by multiplying the two numbers mentioned—will necessarily understate these differences.

References

Anderson, James and Peter Neary. 1991. "A New Approach to Evaluating Trade Policy," World Bank Working Paper. Washington, D.C.: The World Bank.

Anderson, James and Peter Neary. 1994. "Measuring the Restrictiveness of Trade Policy," *World Bank Economic Review* 8:151–169.

Baldwin, Richard E. 1994. *Towards an Integrated Europe*. London: Centre for Economic Policy Research.

Baldwin, Robert E. 1975. *Foreign Trade Regimes and Economic Development: The Philippines*. New York: Columbia University Press.

Baldwin, Robert E. 1982. "The Inefficacy of Trade Policy," Princeton University, International Finance Section, Department of Economics, *Essays in International Finance*, No. 150.

Baldwin, Robert E. 1989. "Measuring Nontariff Trade Policies," National Bureau of Economic Research, Working Paper No. 2978.

Baldwin, Robert E. and J. David Richardson. 1972. "Government Purchasing Policies, Other NTBs, and the International Monetary Crisis," in H. English and K. Hay (eds.), *Obstacles to Trade in the Pacific Area*. Ottawa: Carleton School of International Affairs.

Berry, Steven, James Levinsohn, and Ariel Pakes. 1995. "Voluntary Export Restraints on Automobiles: Evaluating a Strategic Trade Policy," in process.

Bhagwati, Jagdish N. and T. N. Srinivasan. 1975. *Foreign Trade Regimes and Economic Development: India*. New York: Columbia University Press.

Bhagwati, Jagdish N. and T. N. Srinivasan. 1980. "Revenue Seeking: A Generalization of the Theory of Tariffs," *Journal of Political Economy* 88:1069–87.

Brown, Drusilla K., Alan V. Deardorff, Alan K. Fox, and Robert M. Stern. 1996. "The Liberalization of Services Trade: Potential Impacts in the Aftermath of the Uruguay Round," in Will Martin and L. Alan Winters (eds.), *The Uruguay Round and the Developing Economies*. Cambridge: Cambridge University Press.

Campbell, Ken and Richard Cossette. 1994. "A Study of Canada's Non-Tariff Trade Barriers: The Tariff Equivalents of Quantitative Import Restrictions," Research Branch, Canadian International Trade Tribunal (July).

Chapman, Audrey and Po-Yee Lee. 1995. "Canadian & International Use of Anti-Dumping and Countervailing Measures," Research Branch, Canadian International Trade Tribunal (July).

Commission of the European Communities. 1988. *European Economy: The Economics of 1992*. Luxembourg: Office for the Official Publications of the European Communities.

Corden, W. Max. 1966. "The Structure of a Tariff System and the Effective Protective Rate," *Journal of Political Economy* 74:221–37.

Deardorff, Alan V. 1987. "Why Do Governments Prefer Nontariff Barriers?" *Carnegie-Rochester Conference Series on Public Policy* 26:191–216.

Deardorff, Alan V. 1998. "Determinants of Bilateral Trade: Does Gravity Work in a Neoclassical World?" in Jeffrey Frankel, ed., *The Regionalization of the World Economy*, University of Chicago Press.

Deardorff, Alan V. and Robert M. Stern. 1985. "Methods of Measurement of Nontariff Barriers," United Nations Conference on Trade and Development, UNCTAD/ST/MD/28. Geneva: United Nations.

Deltas, George and Simon Evenett. 1997. "Quantitative Estimates of the Effects of Preference Policies," in Bernard M. Hoekman and Petros C. Mavroidis (eds.), *Law and Policy in Public Purchasing: The WTO Agreement on Government Procurement*. Ann Arbor: University of Michigan Press.

Dixon, P. B., B. R. Parmenter, J. Sutton, and D. Vincent. 1982. *ORANI: A Multisectoral Model of the Australian Economy*. Amsterdam: North-Holland Publishing Company.

Eurostat. 1988. *Purchasing Power Parities and Gross Domestic Product in Real Terms: Results 1985*. Luxembourg: Office for the Official Publications of the European Communities.

Faehn, Taran. 1996. "Quantifying Trade Barriers for the Purpose of an ERP Analysis," Statistics Norway, Research Department, processed.

Feenstra, Robert C. 1984. "Voluntary Export Restraints in U.S. Autos, 1980–81: Quality, Employment, and Welfare Effects," in Robert E. Baldwin and Anne O. Krueger (eds.), *The Structure and Evolution of Recent U.S. Trade Policy*. Chicago: University of Chicago Press.

Francois, Joseph F., Hugh M. Arce, Kenneth A. Reinert, and Joseph E. Flynn. 1996. "Commercial Policy and the Domestic Carrying Trade," *Canadian Journal of Economics* 29:181-98.

Francois, Joseph F., Douglas Nelson, and N. David Palmeter. 1997. "Public Procurement in the United States: A Post-Uruguay Round Perspective," in Bernard M. Hoekman and Petros C. Mavroidis (eds.), *Law and Policy in Public Purchasing: The WTO Agreement on Government Procurement*. Ann Arbor: University of Michigan Press.

Glismann, Hans H. 1996. "Economic Effects of Quantitative Import Restrictions in Germany: Summary," Kiel Institute of World Economics. Complete version of study: *Wirtschaftliche Auswirkungen mengenmäfliger Importbeschränkugen* (Kiel, January).

Goldstein, Morris and Mohsin S. Khan. 1984. "Income and Price Effects in Foreign Trade," in Ronald W. Jones and Peter B. Kenen (eds.), *Handbook of International Economics*, Vol. II. Amsterdam: North-Holland Publishing Company.

Greenaway, D. et al. 1995. "Anti-Dumping Policy and Non-Tariff Barriers," A Report to H.M. Treasury and the Department of Trade and Industry for the OECD Pilot Group Meeting on 28 September 1995, Department of Economics, University of Nottingham, processed.

Hardin, Alexis and Leanne Holmes. 1997. *Services Trade and Foreign Direct Investment*, Industry Commission Staff Research Paper (November). Canberra: Australian Government Publishing Services.

Hathaway, Dale E. and Merlinda Ingco. 1996. "Agricultural Liberalization and the Uruguay Round," in Will Martin and L. Alan Winters (eds.), *The Uruguay Round and the Developing Economies*. New York: Cambridge University Press.

Hoekman, Bernard M. 1997. "Evaluating Global Procurement Markets and Multilateral Rules: Data Needs and Availability," in Bernard M. Hoekman and Petros C. Mavroidis (eds.), *Law and Policy in Public Purchasing: The WTO Agreement on Government Procurement*. Ann Arbor: University of Michigan Press.

Hoekman, Bernard 1995. "Assessing the General Agreement on Trade in Services," in Will Martin and L. Alan Winters (eds.), *The Uruguay Round and the Developing Economies*, World Bank Discussion Paper 307, pp. 327-64. Washington, DC: The World Bank. Revised version published in Will Martin and L. Alan Winters (eds.), Cambridge: Cambridge University Press.

Hoekman, Bernard and Carlos Primo Braga. 1997. "Protection and Trade in Services: A Survey." *Open Economies Review* 8:285-308.

Hoekman, Bernard and Michael Kostecki. 1995. *The Political Economy of the World Trading System: From GATT to WTO*. New York/Oxford: Oxford University Press.

Holmoy, Erling and Torbjorn Haegeland. 1995. "Effective Rates of Assistance for Norwegian Industries," Research Department, Statistics Norway, processed.

Hufbauer, Gary Clyde and Kimberley Ann Elliott. 1994. *Measuring the Costs of Protection in the United States*. Washington, D.C.: Institute for International Economics.

Industry Commission, Structural Policy Division, Commonwealth of Australia. 1994. "Pilot Group on NTBs Comments on Canadian Papers and Material on Australia's Own Practices and an Inventory of Relevant Studies," processed (June 21).

Industry Commission, Commonwealth of Australia. 1995. *Assistance to Agricultural and Manufacturing Industries*. Canberra: Australian Government Publishing Service.

Jackson, John H. 1984. "Perspectives on the Jurisprudence of International Trade," *American Economic Review, Papers and Proceedings* 74:277–81.

Jager, H. and G.J. Lanjouw. 1977. "An Alternative Method for Quantifying International Trade Barriers," *Weltwirtschaftliches Archiv* 113 (Heft 4):719–40.

Krueger, Anne O. 1974. "The Political Economy of the Rent Seeking Society," *American Economic Review* 64:291–303.

Laird, Sam. 1996. "Quantifying Commercial Policies," in Joseph F. Francois and Kenneth A. Reinert (eds.), *Applied Methods for Trade Policy Analysis*. New York: Cambridge University Press.

Laird, Sam and Alexander Yeats. 1990. *Quantitative Methods for Trade Barrier Analysis*. London and New York: Macmillan Press, Ltd. and New York University Press.

Laird, Sam and Rene Vossenar. 1991. "Porqué nos preocupan las bareras no arancelarias?" *Información Comercial Española*, Special Issue on Non-tariff Barriers (November).

Leamer, Edward E. 1990a. "Latin America as a Target of Trade Barriers Erected by the Major Developed Countries in 1983," *Journal of Development Economics* 32:337–68.

Leamer, Edward E. 1990b. "The Structure and Effects of Tariffs and Nontariff Barriers in 1983," in Ronald W. Jones and Anne O. Krueger (eds.), *The Political Economy of International Trade*. Cambridge, MA: Basil Blackwell, Inc.

Leamer, Edward E. and Robert M. Stern. 1970. *Quantitative International Economics*. Boston: Allyn and Bacon.

Lester, John and Tony Morehen. 1988. "Trade Barriers Between Canada and the United States," Economic Studies and Policy Analysis Division, Fiscal Policy and Economic Analysis Branch, Department of Finance, Government of Canada, Working Paper No. 88–3.

Linkins, Linda A. and Hugh M. Arce. 1994. "Estimating Tariff Equivalents of Nontariff Barriers," U.S. International Trade Commission, Office of Economics, Working Paper No. 94-06-A.

Lloyd, Tim, Oliver Morrissey, and Geoffrey Reed. 1988. "Estimating the Impact of Anti-Dumping and anti-Cartel Actions Using Intervention Analysis," *Economic Journal* 108:458-76.

Lowinger, Thomas. 1976. "Discrimination in Government Procurement of Foreign Goods in the U.S. and Western Europe," *Southern Economic Journal* 42:451–60.

Martin, Will and L. Alan Winters (eds.). 1996. *The Uruguay Round and the Developing Economies*. Cambridge: Cambridge University Press.

Melchior, Arne. 1993. *Helping Your Industry at the Greatest Cost: The Story of Norwegian Textile Quotas*. Norwegian Institute of International Affairs, Research Report No. 171 (September).

Messerlin, Patrick. 1988. "Experiences of Developing Countries with Antidumping Laws," The World Bank, processed.

Moroz, Andrew W. and Stephen L. Brown. 1987. "Grant Support and Trade Protection for Canadian Industries," Report for the Department of Finance, the Department of External Affairs, and the Department of Regional Industrial Expansion, Government of Canada (April), processed.

OECD. 1986. *The Concept and Measurement of Producer Subsidy Equivalents and Consumer Subsidy Equivalents*. Joint Working Party of the Committee for Agriculture and the Trade Committee (October). Paris: OECD.

OECD Secretariat. 1995. Working Party No. 1 of the Economic Policy Committee Ad Hoc Group of Experts on Indicators of Government Assistance, "Patterns and Pervasiveness of Tariff and Non-Tariff Barriers to Trade in OECD Member Countries," ECO/CPE/WP1/GE(96)3 (June 12).

Pacific Economic Cooperation Council (PECC). 1995. *Survey of Impediments to Trade and Investment in the APEC Region*. Singapore: PECC.

Petri, Peter A. 1997. "Foreign Direct Investment in a Computable General Equilibrium Framework," prepared for Conference, "Making APEC Work: Economic Challenges and Policy Alternatives," Keio University (March 12-14).

Roningen, Vernon O. and Alexander J. Yeats. 1976. "Nontariff Distortions of International Trade: Some Preliminary Evidence," *Weltwirtshcaftliches Archiv* 112 (Heft 4):613–25.

Sampson, Gary and Richard Snape. 1980. "Effects of the EEC's Variable Levies," *Journal of Political Economy* 88:1026–40.

Sampson, Gary and Alexander J. Yeats. 1976. "Do Import Levies Matter? The Case of Sweden," *Journal of Political Economy* 84:881–92.

Sampson, Gary and Alexander J. Yeats. 1977. "An Evaluation of the Common Agricultural Policy as a Barrier Facing Agricultural Exports to the European Economic Community," *American Journal of Agricultural Economics*, 59:99–106.

Saxonhouse, Gary R. 1977. "Regressions from Samples Having Different Characteristics," *Review of Economics and Statistics* 59:234–37.

Saxonhouse, Gary R. and Robert M. Stern. 1989. "Trade and Investment Patterns and Barriers in the United States, Canada, and Japan," in Robert M. Stern (ed.), *Trade and Investment Relations Among the United States, Canada, and Japan*. Chicago: University of Chicago Press.

Sazanami, Yoko, Shujiro Urata, and Hiroki Kawai. 1995. *Measuring the Costs of Protection in Japan*. Washington, D.C.: Institute for International Economics.

Sheikh, Munir and Louis Beausejour. 1995. "Measuring Tariff-Equivalents of Non-Tariff Barriers," Department of Finance, Government of Canada (January), processed.

Stern, Robert M., Jonathan Francis, and Bruce Schumacher. 1976. *Price Elasticities in International Trade*. London: Macmillan Press, Ltd.

Tarr, David G. 1994. "The Welfare Costs of Price Controls for Cars and Color Televisions in Poland: Contrasting Estimates of Rent-Seeking from Recent Experience," *The World Bank Economic Review* 8: 415-43.

United Nations Conference on Trade and Development (UNCTAD). 1996. *World Investment Report 1996: Investment, Trade, and International Policy Arrangements*. New York and Geneva: United Nations.

U.S. International Trade Commission. 1993. *The Economic Effects of Significant U.S. Import Restraints*, Investigation No. 332-325, Publication 2699. Washington, D.C.: USITC.

U.S. International Trade Commission. 1995. *The Economic Effects of Significant U.S. Import Restraints: First Biannual Update*, Investigation No. 332-325, Publication 2935. Washington, D.C.: USITC.

U.S. Tariff Commission. 1974. *Trade Barriers: An Overview*. TC Publication 665. Washington, D.C.: U.S. Government Printing Office.

White, Lawrence J. 1988. *International Trade in Ocean Shipping Services: The United States and the World*. Cambridge: Ballinger for the American Enterprise Institute.

Wisecarver, Daniel. 1974. "The Social Costs of Input-Market Distortions," *American Economic Review* 64: 359-72.

APPENDIX 1

Major Categories of Nontariff Measures and Related Policies

I. Quantitative restrictions and similar specific limitations

1. Import quotas	Restrictions on quantity and/or value of imports of specific commodities for some given time period; administered globally, selectively, or bilaterally.
2. Export limitations	Same as above but with reference to exports.
3. Licensing	Some system of licensing is required to administer the foregoing restrictions. Licensing may be discretionary and also used for statistical purposes.
4. Voluntary export restraints	Restrictions imposed by importing country but administered by exporting country; administered multilaterally and bilaterally; requires system of licensing; essentially similar to an orderly marketing arrangement.
5. Exchange and other financial controls	Restrictions on receipts and/or payments of foreign exchange designed to control international trade and/ or capital movements; will generally require some system of licensing; may involve multiple exchange rates for different kinds of transactions.
6. Prohibitions	May be selective with respect to commodities and countries of origin/destination; includes embargoes; may carry legal sanctions.
7. Domestic content and mixing requirements	Requires that an industry use a certain proportion of domestically produced components and/or materials and labor in producing final products.
8. Discriminatory bilateral agreements	Preferential trading arrangements that may be selective by commodity and country; includes preferential sourcing arrangements.
9. Countertrade	Arrangements involving barter, counterpurchases of goods, and payments in kind.

II. Nontariff charges and related policies affecting imports

1. Variable levies	Based on a target domestic price of imports, a levy is imposed so that the price of imports reaches the target price whatever the cost of imports.

2. Advance deposit requirement	Some proportion of the value of imports must be deposited in advance of the payment, with no allowance for any interest accrued on the deposit.
3. Antidumping duties	Imposition of a special import duty when the price of imports is alleged to lie below the price charged by the foreign firm in its domestic market, or below some measure of its costs of production; minimum foreign prices may be established to "trigger" antidumping investigations and actions.
4. Countervailing duties	Imposition of a special import duty to counteract an alleged foreign government subsidy to production or exports; normally required that domestic injury be shown.
5. Border tax adjustments	When indirect (e.g., sales or value added) taxes are levied on the destination principle, imports will be subject to such taxes but exports will be exempt; the effects on trade will be neutral except in cases in which the adjustments more than compensate for the taxes imposed or exempted, or when the size of the tax differs across commodities.

III. Government participation in trade, restrictive practices, and more general government policies

1. Subsidies and other aids	Direct and indirect subsidies to export and importcompeting industries, including tax benefits, credit concessions, and bilateral tied aid programs.
2. Government procurement policies	Preferences given to domestic over foreign firms in bidding on public-procurement contracts, including explicit cost differentials and informal procedures favoring procurement from domestic firms.
3. State trading, government monopolies, and exclusive franchises	Government actions which may result in trade distortions, including government-sanctioned, discriminatory international transport agreements.
4. Government industrial policy and regional development measures	Government actions designed to aid particular firms, industrial sectors, and regions to adjust to changes in market conditions.
5. Government financed research and development and other technology policies	Government actions designed to correct market distortions and aid private firms; includes policies relating to intellectual property (patents, copyrights, and trademarks) and technological spillovers from government programs, such as defense and public health.
6. National systems of taxation and social insurance	Personal and corporate income taxation, unemployment insurance, social security, and

	related policies which may have an impact on trade.
7. Macroeconomic policies	Monetary/fiscal, balance-of-payments, and exchangerate actions which have an impact on national output, foreign trade, and capital movements.
8. Competition policies	Antitrust and related policies (e.g., intellectual property regulations) designed to foster or restrict competition and which may have an impact on foreign trade and investment.
9. Foreign investment policies	Screening and monitoring of inward and/or outward foreign direct investment, including performance requirements affecting production and trade.
10. Foreign corruption policies	Policies designed to prohibit or restrict bribes and related practices in connection with foreign trade and investment.
11. Immigration policies	General or selective policies designed to limit or encourage international movement of labor and which have an impact on foreign trade and investment.

IV. Customs procedures and administrative practices

1. Customs valuation procedures	Use of specially constructed measures of price rather than the invoice or transactions price for the purpose of levying tariffs.
2. Customs classification procedures	Use of national methods of customs classification rather than an internationally harmonized method for the purpose of levying tariffs.
3. Customs clearance procedures	Documentation, inspection, and related practices which may impede trade.

V. Technical barriers to trade

1. Health and sanitary regulations and quality standards	Technical regulations designed for domestic objectives but which may discriminate against imports.
2. Safety and industrial standards and regulations	See above.
3. Packaging and labeling regulations, including trademarks	See above.
4. Advertising and media regulations	See above.

Source: Adapted from Deardorff and Stern (1985, pp. 13-14).

APPENDIX 2

Illustrative Measures of the Nominal and Effective Rates of Assistance

Calculation of the Nominal Rate of Assistance (NRA) and Effective Rate of Assistance (ERA)

The component measures for calculating the nominal rate of assistance or output (NRA) and nominal rate of assistance on materials (NRM) are noted in tables A.2.1 and A.2.2.

While subject to some limiting assumptions noted in our earlier discussion, calculation of ERAs provides potentially very useful information on the incentive effects that a variety of government policies may have on the allocation of capital, labor, and land across different sectors. In table A.2.3, we provide an illustration of a calculation of the ERA for the Australian iron and steel industry for the mid-1980s that indicates the type of information required and the steps in calculating the ERA.

TABLE A.2.1. Component Measures Included in Calculation of the Nominal Rate of Assistance on Output (NRA) and the Nominal Rate of Assistance on Materials (NRM)

Component Measures of NRA and NRM

1. **Measures which alter output returns**
   - tariffs
   - quantitative import restrictions
   - domestic pricing arrangements
   - export subsidies or taxes
   - export facilitation arrangements
   - local content schemes
   - production subsidies
2. **Measures which alter intermediate input costs**
   - tariffs
   - commodity taxes
   - input subsidies
   - local content schemes

3. Measures that alter returns from using resources in particular sectors

concessional credit
income tax concessions
special depreciation allowances
special employment allowances

Calculation of NRA

The output assistance provided by Government interventions is the increase in the gross returns from production above that which would apply in the absence of assistance. The gross return from production with assistance is called the assisted value of production (AP). The (hypothetical) gross return from that production without assistance is called the unassisted value of production (UP). The increase in the gross returns is called the gross subsidy equivalent (GSE). It is the notional amount of money that would give the same amount of assistance to gross returns as is provided by the existing government interventions.

GSE = AP - UP

The Nominal Rate of Assistance on outputs (NRA) is the percentage increase in gross returns per unit of output, relative to the (hypothetical) situation of no assistance.

NRA = (GSE/UP) * 100

Some interventions assist by raising prices (for example, tariffs), while others increase returns without increasing prices (for example, production subsidies).

Calculation of NRM

Intermediate inputs are a cost of production. Government interventions, such as tariffs, typically raise these costs. The cost of intermediate inputs with assistance is called the assisted value of intermediate inputs (AM). The (hypothetical) cost of those intermediate inputs without assistance is called the unassisted value of intermediate inputs (UM). The increase in the cost of intermediate inputs is called the tax equivalent on intermediate inputs (TEM), or sometimes just tax on materials. It is the notional amount of tax that would increase the cost of intermediate inputs by the same amount as the existing government interventions.

TEM = AM - UM

The nominal rate of assistance on intermediate inputs (or materials) (**NRM**) is the percentage increase in the cost of intermediate inputs per unit of input relative to the (hypothetical) situation of no assistance.

NRM = (TEM/UM) * 100

Some interventions raise the price of intermediate inputs (for example, tariffs) and some lower their cost (for example, subsidies to users). Measures which assist the production of intermediate inputs without altering their price to user industries (for example, production subsidies) are not included.

Source: Industry Commission (1995, pp. 5-6 and 45-46).

TABLE A.2.2. Calculation of the Effective Rate of Assistance (ERA)

Value Added Assistance

The assistance effects of government interventions that directly and specifically target land, labour or capital returns in particular activities may be measured as the notional amount of money, or subsidy equivalent, necessary to yield the same increase in returns to the land, labour or capital used in the activity or industry, as is provided by the assistance. This is called the Subsidy to Value Adding Factors (SVA). Interventions that apply generally to the use of resources throughout an economy (for example, income and value added taxes) are not included.

Net Assistance and the Effective Rate of Assistance (ERA)

The net assistance effect of government interventions on the use of resources in an activity, or an industry, may be measured by the notional amount of money, or subsidy equivalent, necessary to provide the same increase in returns to value adding factors as is provided by the existing structure of assistance. The return to value adding factors, including the effect of assistance, is called the assisted value added (AVA). The (hypothetical) return to those value adding factors without assistance is called the unassisted valued added (UVA). The increase in returns to value adding factors is called the Net Subsidy Equivalent (NSE) and may be derived by adding up output assistance and value added assistance, and subtracting the tax from intermediate input assistance.

$$NSE = AVA - UVA \text{ or}$$
$$= GSE - TEM = GSA$$

The Effective Rate of Assistance (ERA) is the percentage increase in returns, to an activity's, or industry's, value added per unit of output, relative to the (hypothetical) situation of no assistance.

$$ERA = (NSE/UVA) * 100$$

Source: Industry Commission (1995, pp. 46-47).

TABLE A.2.3. Illustrative Calculation of an Effective Rate of Assistance (ERA) for the Australian Iron and Steel Industry for the Mid-1980s

	Calculation	Value (A$m)	Data Source
	Value of output	5174.0	Sales and transfers out (adjusted for selling and distribution expenses) for the 3-digit ASIC (Australian Standard Industrial Classification) 'Basic iron and steel' industry from the manufacturing census conducted by the Australian Bureau of Statistics (ABS).
•	Production subsidies	19.3	Subsidies paid to producers of goods comprising the 3-digit 'Basic iron and steel' industry. Data taken from government budget papers.
•	Export incentives	1.6	Export incentives paid for market development and promotion to producers of 'Basic iron and steel'. Data from government budget papers and the Board responsible for administering the Schemes.
•	Special labour adjustment	2.0	Payments made under special Government plan for restructuring the industry.
(1)	Assisted value of output (AP)	5194.9	Value of output plus the value of subsidies and export incentives.
(2)	Less inputs (AM)	3364.7	Materials and fuels used by 3-digit ASIC industry 'Basic iron and steel' from the manufacturing census conducted by the ABS.
(3)	Assisted Value Added (AVA)	1832.2	AP–AM+SVA=AVA
Output assistance			
•	Tariffs	406.2	The subsidy equivalent of tariffs derived from General tariff rates applying to competing imports of 'Basic iron and steel.' Requires the construction of a concordance between 'Basic iron and steel' product groups (used by the ABS to collect manufacturing census data) and the Customs tariff – the GSE for each product group is derived by subtracting from each group's value of output, its 'unassisted' value. The unassisted value is estimated by deflating each group's assisted value of output by its average nominal tariff rate. The GSE for the 'Basic iron and steel' industry is the summation of each product groups' GSE.

•	Production subsidies	19.3	(from above)
•	Export incentives	1.6	(from above)
(4)	Gross Subsidy Equivalent (GSE)	427.1	Subsidy equivalent of tariffs + Production subsidies + Export incentives
(5)	Unassisted Value of Output (UP)	4767.8	AP–GSE=UP

Nominal rate of assistance on output (NRA)
NRA=100*(4)/(5)=9.0 percent

	Intermediate input assistance		
•	Tariffs on materials	208.3	The TEM of tariffs derived from General tariff rates (adjusted for concessional tariff entry of imported inputs) applying to competing imports of material and fuel inputs used in the 'Basic iron and steel' industry. Requires the construction of a concordance between 'Basic iron and steel' material group (used by the ABS to collect manufacturing census data) and the Customs tariff. The TEM for each material group is derived by subtracting from each group's assisted value of materials and fuels used, its 'unassisted' value (estimated by deflating each group's assisted value by its average nominal tariff rate). The TEM for the 'Basic iron and steel' industry is the summation of each material group's TEM.
(6)	Tax Equivalent on Intermediate Inputs (TEM)	208.3	
(7)	Unassisted value of Intermediate Inputs (UM)	3156.4	(2)-(6) AM–TEM=UM

Nominal rate of assistance on intermediate inputs (NRM)
NRM=100*(6)/(7)=6.6 percent

	Valued added assistance		
(8)	Subsidy to value added (SVA)	2.0	Payment for special labour adjustment. Data from government budget papers.

(9)	Unassisted Value Added (UVA)	1611.4	(5)-(7) UP–UM=UVA
(10)	Net Subsidy Equivalent (NSE)	220.8	(3)-(9) or (4)-(6)+(8) AVA–UVA or GSE–TEM+SVA

Effective rate of assistance (ERA)
ERA=100*(10)/(9)=14 percent

Source: Industry Commission (1995, pp. 58-60).

APPENDIX 3

Formulas for Measuring NTBs

Note Regarding Country Size:

In all of the formulas of this appendix, the notation represents prices, costs, etc., that prevail in an equilibrium in the presence of NTBs, and there is no assumption that any of these would necessarily remain the same if the NTBs were removed. Thus the formulas can be applied equally well to a country that is large enough for its trade to influence world prices as to a country that is too small to have such an effect.

Notation:

For a good that is not traded:

MC	= Marginal cost in production
r_p	= Producer rent (markup over marginal cost)
$P_e = MC + r_p$	= Ex-factory price
C_w	= Cost of wholesale distribution
$P_w = P_e + C_w$	= Wholesale price
C_r	= Cost of retail distribution
$P_r = P_w + C_r$	= Retail price
$C_d = C_w + C_r$	= Total cost of distribution

Thus: $P_r = P_e + C_d = MC + r_p + C_d$

For a good that is traded:

MC	= Marginal cost in production
r_p	= Producer rent (may include some rent from NTB)
$P_e = MC + r_p$	= Ex-factory price
C_s	= Cost of getting good from factory onto ship
r_x	= Exporting-country post-factory rent per unit of NTB, built into f.o.b. price (ad valorem $\rho_x = r_x/P_c$)
$P_f = P_e + C_s + r_x$	= F.o.b. price
C_t	= Cost of transport and insurance
$P_c = P_f + C_t$	= C.i.f. price
t	= Tariff in specific terms (ad valorem $\tau = t/P_c$)

r_m = Importing-country rent per unit of NTB (ad valorem $\rho_m = r_m/P_c$)

$P_i = P_c + t + r_m$ = "Inside border" price

$= P_c + (\tau + \rho_m)P_c = (1 + \tau + \rho_m)(P_f + C_t)$

C_w = Cost of wholesale distribution

$P_w = P_i + C_w$ = Wholesale price

C_r, C_d, P_r = Same as for nontraded good

Thus $P_r = P_e + C_s + r_x + C_t + t + r_m + C_d$

$= MC + r_p + C_s + r_x + C_t + t + r_m + C_d$

Thus an NTB, by creating rents $r = r_x + r_m$ (plus a portion of r_p in some cases), drives a wedge between marginal cost, *MC*, and the inside-border price, P_i, analogous to a tariff. The tariff equivalent, *TE*, of the NTB, as we define it, is the *ad valorem* tariff that, if it replaced the NTB, would lead to the same value of this inside-border price (or, for some NTBs that are thought to work by making distribution more difficult, that lead to the same wholesale or retail price, adjusted for any legitimate differences in distribution costs). In ad valorem terms relative to the c.i.f. price,[1] if rents from the NTB change prices in the same way as a tariff of the same size, then the tariff equivalent of the NTB is

$$TE = \rho = \frac{r}{P_c} = \frac{r_x + r_m}{P_c}$$

The problem is to infer these rents (to the extent that they do alter prices) from other information and assumptions. Note that since the c.i.f. price and tariff are observable, a part of this problem—the measurement of rents in the importing country, r_m—would be trivial if the inside-border price were observable. To an extent, therefore, the problem of measuring the *TE* is the problem of measuring this inside-border price.

In the formula above, as in all those below, we measure *TE* as a fraction. All of the formulas should be multiplied by 100 to obtain percentages.

All of the prices and costs above, if they carry a superscript, *m*, will refer to the imported good whose tariff equivalent is being sought. Other superscripts indicate other goods, as follows (examples show retail prices, but other costs and prices for the same goods are indicated similarly).

P_r^m = Retail price of imported good

P_r^d = Retail price of domestic comparable good ($P_r^d = P_r^m$ if they are perfect substitutes)

P_r^x = Retail price of import good in another export market

P_r^o = Retail price of import good in exporter's own domestic market

All prices and costs are expressed in importing country's currency at the prevailing exchange rate.

Formulas: Motivation and Application

I. Import Quotas

A. If quotas are auctioned

1. If the auction is plausibly competitive, the auction price per unit of quota $A = r$ and can be used to measure the *TE*:

$$TE^{AUC} = \frac{A}{P_c} \qquad \text{(I.A.1)}$$

If bids are stated in ad valorem rather than specific form, then the bid itself is the tariff equivalent. In both cases, care should be taken to observe variations in auction prices across time, and to use a suitable average of prices for a period of time. If an auction at the beginning of a time period is followed by secondary market sales at transfer prices different from the auction price, then these transfer prices should be used, also averaged over time, rather than just the auction price.

If the unit of the auction is not a one-time unit of import quota, but a recurring right to import a unit each year for a period of years, then it is necessary to convert the auction price to a price per unit of one-time quota using a discount rate that takes account of both the interest rate and the uncertainty of future trade and quotas. This is sufficiently difficult to do with any accuracy that we recommend not using auction prices at all in this situation.

2. It is possible that auctions may be conducted for the quotas that apply to some exporters of a product, such as Hong Kong, but not others. In that case this method can still be applied to those other exporters if their auction prices can first be inferred from the Hong Kong auction price together with differences in labor costs and productivity between the exporting countries and Hong Kong. Thus, letting P_e^{hk} and P_e^{o} be the ex-factory prices of exports from Hong Kong and the other exporter respectively, it can be assumed that these two prices differ primarily by measurable differences in wages, W^{hk} and W^{o}, and in labor productivity, go^{hk} and go^{o}, measured as gross output per worker. Thus

$$P_e^{o} = \left(\frac{W^{o}}{W^{hk}}\right)\left(\frac{go^{hk}}{go^{o}}\right)P_e^{hk}$$

Assuming that products of the two exporters are perfect substitutes (hence $P_c^{hk} = P_c^o$) and that transport and other distribution costs are also identical, the auction price for the other exporter can be estimated as

$$A^o = A^{hk} + (P_e^{hk} - P_e^o)$$

and this can be used in the formula above for TE^{AUC}. Of course if A^o turns out to be negative in this calculation, then one of the assumptions is evidently incorrect. If A^o is negative and not too large, however, one can probably safely assume that the tariff equivalent for the other country is simply zero.

3. If the auction is thought to be significantly less than perfectly competitive, then the auction price is of no value, except as an indication of how rent is shared with the government. Use the same techniques listed below for quotas that are given away.

B. If quotas are exchanged (transferred) on a plausibly competitive secondary market, use the transfer price in place of A in TE^{AUC} (I.A.), with the same caveats mentioned there.

C. If quotas are allocated to (a large number of) domestic residents (hence r_x =0), and if there are enough sellers in the relevant markets to justify assuming perfect competition, do the following, depending on availability of markets for goods with comparable characteristics or distribution costs:

1. For a good with a perfect domestic substitute (hence $P_r^d = P_r^m$), use comparison of c.i.f. price with ex-factory price of domestic substitute:

$$TE^{SUBST} = \frac{P_e^d - P_c^m}{P_c^m} + \frac{C_d^d - C_d^m}{P_c^m} - \tau \qquad \text{(I.C.1)}$$

Note, that if the import and its perfect substitute on the domestic market are presumed to have the same distribution costs ($C_d^d = C_d^m$), then the tariff equivalent is obtained simply by comparing the ex-factory price of the domestic substitute to the c.i.f. price of the import, and subtracting the ad valorem tariff, τ.

If distribution costs are not the same, then these need to be accounted for as shown. In particular, if the import has higher distribution costs for some reason, this can explain part or all of a gap between the ex-factory and c.i.f. prices, which then do not necessarily indicate the effects of only the quota and tariff.

If an excess distribution cost of the imported good is itself regarded as an NTB (in addition to the quota), then failing to account for it as above will implicitly attribute its effect to the quota. If the concern is the total barrier to trade and not how it is divided between quota and distribution costs, this would be acceptable.

2. If the imported good is a discounted perfect substitute for a domestic good, then the formula above needs to be reduced by the size of the discount. That is, suppose that the import is comparable to the domestic good but is known to sell at a discount due to certain natural disadvantages of imported goods (referred to in Industry Commission 1994 Attachment A, pp. 6-7 as "natural protection"–a discount that covers "a range of uncertainties associated with importing and because of the ease of contacting local suppliers if difficulties arose"–and as "local advantage"). Then if the size of that discount, δ, can be estimated separately from knowledge of the industry, a tariff equivalent can be derived from the same price comparison as above but starting with $P_r^d = P_r^m/(1-\delta)$:

$$TE^{DISC} = TE^{SUBST} - \delta\frac{P_r^d}{P_c^m} \qquad \text{(I.C.2)}$$

3. If a good has no perfect domestic substitute but is itself also exported by the foreign producers to another country where there is no quota, then assuming that foreign producers require the same ex-factory price for both destinations ($P_e^x = P_e^m$), one can infer the tariff equivalent from a comparison of prices at the same stage of distribution (wholesale or retail) across countries, together with differences in distribution costs and tariffs in the two markets. That is,

$$TE^{EXP} = \frac{P_r^m - P_r^x}{P_c^m} - \frac{C^m - C^x}{P_c^m} - \frac{t^m - t^x}{P_c^m} \qquad \text{(I.C.3)}$$

where the unsubscripted C's are the sums ($C_s + C_t + C_d$) of the costs to the two markets. (To use wholesale prices, change P_r to P_w and C_d to C_w.) Thus one can use differences across countries in the same traded good's retail or wholesale prices to indicate the restrictiveness of a quota if distribution costs and tariff costs can be assumed to be the same, or exactly offsetting, along the two routes. And if these costs are different but can be measured, they can be accounted for as indicated. However, if there is no market that is quota-free, this will not work.

If more than one unconstrained foreign market is available for comparison, replace the export prices and costs above with averages across countries. Note also that estimates of C^m and C^x separately are not necessary for this calculation. Only their difference is needed. The expression $C^m - C^x$ can be replaced by an estimate of the difference in distribution costs, so that accuracy in measuring absolute levels of C^m and C^x is not an issue.

4. If a perfect domestic substitute does not exist, but there is an imperfect domestic substitute for which domestic distribution costs are deemed likely to be similar to those of the imported good (or linearly related to those costs, as in $C_d^m = a + bC_d^d$ where a,b are known constants), then

$$TE^{IMP} = \frac{(P_r^m - P_c^m) - [a + b(P_r^d - P_e^d)]}{P_c^m} - \tau \qquad \text{(I.C.4)}$$

Note that if distribution costs are thought to differ, but if that difference is itself regarded as an NTB, then setting a=0 and b=1 above will include that distributional NTB in the measured *TE*, along with the effect of the quota.

If it is not the total distribution costs, $C_d = C_w + C_r$, that are known to be related, but only the wholesale distribution costs, $C_w^m = a + bC_w^d$, then the above equation for *TE* holds with P_w's replacing P_r's.

D. If import quotas are allocated to a small number of domestic residents, so that quota holders have some market power, it may be that they will raise the price of the import above what would be needed to reduce demand only to the level of the quota. In that case, the quota will be underutilized, but this will not mean that the quota has not restricted trade. On the contrary, it has restricted trade more than it would have if the quota holders had been competitive. Each of the methods described above for allocations to a large number of domestic residents (formulas for TE^{SUB}, TE^{EXP}, and TE^{IMP}) will still be valid for measuring the tariff equivalent of the quota. It is important that the exporters of the good be perfectly competitive (so that $P_e^x = P_e^m$ in TE^{EXP}), but otherwise the same formulas apply.

E. If import quotas are allocated to foreigners, then the export prices (P_f and P_c) both include some quota rents as indicated above, and TE^{SUB} and TE^{IMP} that compare to P_c cannot be used.

1. So long as the quotas are not allocated to the foreign producers themselves, and if these producers are competitive, then the formula for TE^{EXP} can still be applied, since the ex-factory prices, P_e, to different destinations would be equal and would not include rents.

2. If quotas are allocated to foreign producers, then formula TE^{EXP} can be adapted if these foreign producers also sell the same product in another NTB-free export market. It will not now be the case that $P_e^x = P_e^m$, since the producers will incorporate their rents from the NTB into their ex-factory price destined for the importing-country market. But if they sell the same product in both markets, then their marginal production costs will be the same, $MC^x = MC^m$. If producers are perfectly competitive without the NTB, then $r_p^x = 0$ and r_p^m is entirely due to the NTB (whether or not the producer is able to raise price above the demand price for the quantity permitted by the quota). These assumptions then again yield the formula for TE^{EXP}.

   If producers are not perfectly competitive, but can be assumed to earn the same monopoly rents per unit in both markets without the quota, so that rents due to the quota are $r = (r_p^m - r_p^x) + r_x^m + r_m^m$, then the same expression holds.

   Note again that the C's in the formula for TE^{EXP} (I.C.3) include all costs, from shipping inside the producing country through retail distribution in the importing and other export markets. Analogous formulas are possible comparing wholesale prices, as before. In addition, if it is certain that all rents from the quota are confined to the producer, then comparisons may also be made between c.i.f. prices, f.o.b. prices, or even ex-factory prices, making appropriate adjustments in the C's and tariffs. The formula in this last case will be the same as TE^{OWN} below with export country replacing own country.

3. If quotas are allocated to foreign producers who do not export to a third country market, but who do sell the same product (with $MC^o = MC^m$) in their own domestic market, and if market power can be assumed the same in both markets absent the quota so that $r = r_p^m - r_p^o$, then the TE can be inferred from a comparison of ex-factory prices to both destinations:

$$TE^{OWN} = \frac{P_e^m - P_e^o}{P_c^m} \tag{I.E.3}$$

   If ex-factory prices are not available, or if quota rents are thought to accrue partly at later stages of distribution, then comparison of own-country and import prices at later stages may be attempted. However, these comparisons require rather detailed data on shipping, transportation, and distribution costs plus tariffs. For example, the formula for comparing retail prices in the own and import markets, assuming $MC^o = MC^m$ and $r = (r_p^m - r_p^o) + r_x^m + r_m^m$, is

$$TE^{OWN^*} = \frac{P_r^m - P_r^o}{P_c^m} - \frac{C_s^m - C_t^m - t}{P_c^m} - \frac{C_d^m - C_d^o}{P_c^m} \qquad \text{(I.E.3*)}$$

None of these additional terms is likely to be negligible, since even the two distribution costs, C_d^m and C_d^o, occur in different countries and are likely to be different. The main hope would be that some other unprotected good with similar costs in both countries might be used as the basis for comparison. This seems sufficiently tenuous that we do not devote space and notation to illustrating the possibility, which would be somewhat analogous to the formula for TE^{IMP} in (I.C.4) above.

F. If the rents due to a quota are thought to be shared by resident individuals or firms in both the exporting country and the importing country, then TE^{EXP}–comparing retail or wholesale prices in the domestic market with another quota-free export market, and taking account of differences in distribution costs and tariffs–can still be used, since it includes rents in both countries.

G. If there are no imports at all under a quota, as in the case of an embargo, then no import price will be observed and none of the above formulas can be applied. Participants in the market may nonetheless know fairly accurately the prices at which imports would be available if there were no restrictions, and thus estimates of c.i.f. and f.o.b. prices in the formula for TE^{SUBST} may still be used. Alternatively, such estimates may be constructed from f.o.b. prices to other export markets and estimates of transportation costs. That is, if $P_f^m = P_f^e$ and goods are perfect substitutes, then

$$TE^{EMBARG} = \frac{P_e^d - P_c^x}{P_c^x} + \frac{C_t^x - C_t^m}{P_c^x} + \frac{C_d^d - C_d^m}{P_c^x} - \tau \qquad \text{(I.G)}$$

If it can be assumed that the embargoed imports would face the same transportation costs to the domestic market as to an existing export market, and that their domestic distribution costs would be the same as domestic goods, then this formula yields a *TE* with only minimal information.

H. Tariff-Quotas: A tariff-quota permits imports in excess of the quota but only at a higher tariff rate, τ* than the rate τ that applies to imports within the quota. If imports in excess of the quota do *not* occur, then the tariff-quota is the same as any other quota. If imports in excess of the quota *do* occur, then the market behaves at the margin as though it were subject only to a tariff, at the higher rate τ*. Thus the tariff equivalent of a tariff-quota cannot exceed τ*. Unless it is known with confidence whether imports above quota have occurred, the *TE* should be measured using the most appropriate of the methods listed above for simple quotas, yielding TE^{QEST} as the estimated *TE* of the quota alone. Then the *TE* of the tariff-quota should be taken as the minimum of that and τ*:

$$TE^{T\text{-}Q} = \min(TE^{QEST}, \tau^*) \qquad \text{(I.H)}$$

II. Variable Levies

Even though the effects of variable levies are in many ways different from those of a quota or a tariff, in terms of the way they change over time as conditions change, the measurement of their tariff equivalent could be quite straightforward as long as the full effect of the variable levy can be assumed to accrue to the importing country government as revenue from the levy itself. The first method below just uses these revenues to measure the average tariff equivalent over a period. On the other hand, if knowledge of the variable levy leads foreign exporters to raise their prices in order to capture some of these rents, then the revenues will understate the *TE*. The second and third methods therefore use comparison prices instead for this purpose.

A. If there is reason to believe that foreign exporters *do not* raise prices in response to the variable levy, then use the revenues from the levy relative to the value of trade to measure its tariff equivalent. Letting *REV* be the revenues collected from the variable levy on a particular product over a period of time, and letting *M* be the f.o.b. value of imports subject to the levy, the tariff equivalent is

$$TE^{VAR1} = \frac{REV}{M} \qquad \text{(II.A)}$$

There is no objective indicator that will tell whether export prices have been raised by a variable levy. However, it seems likely that export prices are more likely to be raised the fewer foreign exporters there are in competition. Thus this formula is best applied when the export market is reasonably competitive.

B. If there is reason to believe that foreign exporters *do* raise prices in response to the variable levy, then use comparisons of f.o.b. prices into the import market with f.o.b. prices into other export markets, together with the levy revenues, to infer the size of the levy.

$$TE^{VAR2} = \frac{P_f^m - P_f^x}{P_c^m} + \frac{REV}{M} \qquad \text{(II.B)}$$

C. Alternatively, if these prices are difficult to observe, one can compare inside-border prices in the import market (which in this case are those prices mandated by the variable levy) with inside border prices in other markets. Assuming that competitive foreign suppliers require the same f.o.b. prices to all destinations ($P_f^x = P_f^m$) except when altered by the variable levy, the latter can be constructed from c.i.f. prices, tariffs, and the difference between transport costs, if there are no NTBs in these other markets:

$$TE^{VAR3} = \frac{P_i^m - P_c^x - t^x}{P_c^x} - \frac{C_t^m - C_t^x}{P_c^x} \qquad \text{(II.C)}$$

III. Voluntary Export Restraints

These are normally implemented as quantitative restrictions, allocated to producers in the exporting country. Their tariff equivalents are given by the same formulas listed above for quotas that are allocated to foreigners.

IV. Government Procurement Regulations

A. If the regulation takes the form of an explicit preference (buy domestic goods unless imports are at least *x%* cheaper), then the tariff equivalent is just the size of that preference times the share of demand (government plus non-government) that is subject to the preference:

$$TE^{GOV1} = x\frac{D_g}{D_p + D_g} \qquad \text{(IV.A)}$$

This also assumes that imports cannot qualify for the preference with only minimal domestic processing. To the extent that is possible, the tariff equivalent is reduced to the percentage excess cost of that processing.

B. If the regulation is only implicit, then it is necessary to estimate the proportion of government expenditures that would have been imported in the absence of the regulation. This is commonly done by comparison with the import share of the same or a comparable category of private expenditure. Let θ_g^m be the import share of government expenditure and θ_p^m be the import share of private expenditure. Then

$$TE^{GOV2} = \left(1 - \frac{\theta_g^m}{\theta_p^m}\right)\left(\frac{D_g}{D_p + D_g}\right)\frac{(1+\tau)}{\eta} \qquad \text{(IV.B)}$$

where τ is the ad valorem nominal tariff rate and η is the (positive) elasticity of demand for imports, to be estimated econometrically or taken from the literature.[2]

V. Countervailing Duties

Countervailing duties (CVDs) are just tariffs, and they can be measured as such. It is true that the threat of a CVD, even if never implemented, might have some effect in restricting trade, but to the extent that this occurs only through a reduction in a countervailable subsidy, it is not clear that this effect should be regarded as an NTB. Likewise, the availability in the law of CVDs and a demonstrated tendency to use them could have a dampening effect on trade. But we know of no obvious way to quantify either of these possible effects.

CVDs should therefore be measured directly from the sizes of the duties as they are levied. The only special concern here is that these duties may not appear in the regular tariff schedules, and therefore it is necessary to look for them directly, in the records of the outcomes of CVD cases.

VI. Anti-Dumping Duties

Anti-dumping duties (ADDs) are similar to CVDs in many, but not all, respects. Because they are levied against private firms instead of governments, they may induce changes in firm behavior that a CVD would not. Thus in addition to simply measuring the ADDs themselves as tariffs, one must also examine any settlements that are reached in AD cases that alter firm behavior in prescribed ways. It is also plausible that the active use of an AD statute by a country will have effects on trade in sectors where actual cases are never filed, and these effects in principle could be large and should be measured, although we know of no general useful way to do this.[3]

A. All duties that are currently being levied as a result of past and present AD cases should be recorded, converted if necessary to ad valorem terms, and included in any general quantification of NTBs. If these duties have already been included along with other tariffs, then they must not be double-counted. But it is desirable to separate them from other tariffs because they have somewhat different effects. (An ordinary tariff will normally, like any tax, be absorbed partially by the exporting firm or industry. However, exporters that are subject to an ADD know that if they lower price at all, the dumping margin and the ADD itself will simply be increased. Thus the true tariff equivalent of an ADD in terms of its effect on the domestic price of imports is somewhat larger than the size of the duty itself. However, the extent of this understatement is difficult to know, since it requires knowledge about market size and structure that is not readily available. We therefore recommend that ADDs be reported in terms of the simple ad valorem duties that are levied, but that they be reported separately from other tariffs.)

In order to include all current ADDs, note that it is necessary to examine not only AD cases from the current year, but also cases going back arbitrarily far in time since, under current WTO rules, ADDs can be renewed indefinitely if removal would cause material injury. It would be best if countries would maintain an inventory of all AD cases, including all for which ADDs are still being levied, and then update that inventory each year.

B. All AD cases should be examined for this purpose, not just those that have led to a positive determination and the levying of a duty. All cases that were settled prior to a final determination should also be included, and the nature of any settlement should be quantified and included in the measure of AD as an NTB. Such settlements can take many forms, and their quantification will seldom be straightforward. The following are two examples that could be used as guides to actual cases:

   1. If the settlement takes the form of a "price undertaking," in which the foreign exporter agrees to keep price at some higher level, a comparison of the promised price with recent past prices will yield a percentage difference that can be taken as the *TE* of the undertaking.

   2. If the settlement takes the form of a "quantity undertaking" or a "market share undertaking," in which the foreign exporter agrees in some fashion to limit sales in the domestic market, this can be quantified with an elasticity approach. First calculate the percentage reduction in quantity of exports to which the exporter has agreed, say $\%\Delta M$. The let the *TE* be the percentage price increase that would reduce demand for the good by that amount. That is, assuming a (positive) elasticity of demand of η,

$$TE^{SET} = \frac{\%\Delta M}{\eta} \qquad \text{(VI.B.2)}$$

C. While there is no general way to infer the trade reducing effects of a whole complex of AD laws in many countries, it is possible that if a particular country and sector is suspected of being especially prone to AD actions, the resulting discouraging effect on trade may be picked up by using price comparisons. Since exporters to that country would be hesitant to charge low prices, a comparison of export prices to other export prices destined for other country markets may reveal a differential. If so, then the formula for TE^{EXP} in (I.C.4) will provide the tariff equivalent.

VII. Domestic Content Requirements

Domestic content requirements can take many forms, and it is therefore essential that they be examined closely to determine exactly how they are constructed and what effects they are likely to have. Our analysis follows Industry Commission (1995, pp. 91-93).

A. A content requirement typically says that some percentage, c, of a good's content that must be sourced domestically, in return for which the firm producing the good will be given some benefit. If the firm opts not to satisfy the requirement, then the requirement has had no effect at all. Similarly, if the firm opts to include more than c percent of domestic content in its product, then again the requirement has had no effect. Only if the firm satisfies the requirement and finds it binding, has the requirement had any protective effect (on the input industry). Thus the first step in quantifying the effects of content requirement schemes is to identify those cases in which this is true.

B. Let b be the benefit given to the firm if it satisfies the requirement, per unit quantity of its output, and let C be its cost per unit in the presence of the local content requirement. To the extent that the content requirement is binding, it raises the cost of domestic inputs by some percent, TE, which is therefore the tariff equivalent of the content requirement. (That is, if a tariff of TE had been levied on all such inputs, their domestically-produced substitutes would have risen in price by this amount.) For the using firm to break even while satisfying the requirement, the increased cost of these inputs, $CcTE/(1+TE)$, must be equal to the benefit provided:

$$b = \frac{TE}{1+TE} cC$$

Thus

$$TE^{CON1} = \frac{b}{cC - b} = \frac{\beta}{c - \beta} \qquad \text{(VII.B)}$$

where $\beta = b/C$ is the benefit expressed in *ad valorem* terms.

C. In the case considered by the Industry Commission, satisfying the content requirement entitles the using firm to import its remaining inputs tariff-free. Letting t be the percentage tariff on inputs, the benefit from satisfying the content requirement is a reduction in cost of $t/(1+t)$ on its inputs (the fraction $(1-c)$ are now tariff free, and the tariff on the fraction c has been replaced by the cost of domestic inputs included in the TE), or $b=tC/(1+t)$. Thus

$$TE^{CON2} = \frac{t}{c(1+t) - t} \qquad \text{(VII.C)}$$

VIII. Customs Valuation Procedures

In order for a country's tariff rates to be comparable to those of other countries, they should be calculated as a percentage of the f.o.b. price of the import, and this f.o.b. price should be based on a free-market transaction. If imports are valued on any other basis for the application of ad valorem tariffs, then the difference can be viewed as an NTB. Since the Customs Valuation Code of the Tokyo Round, however, countries have foresworn the arbitrary use of valuation procedures in order to restrict trade, and the extent to which such procedures currently cause problems is primarily a result of the difficulty of estimating free-market prices for goods that do not themselves go through markets, such as intra-firm trade. Such difficulties will typically make it equally difficult to calculate the size of the implicit NTB that may be present, and therefore it is not expected that customs valuation procedures will, for most countries, constitute a major source of measurable NTBs. The formulas that we give here, therefore, are not expected to be widely used.

A. If valuation procedures are well defined, but do not accord with the standard of valuing at the f.o.b. free-market price, then the preferred method of dealing with them is not to calculate any NTB at all, but rather to recalculate the true ad valorem tariff rates relative to f.o.b. free-market prices.

B. If for some reason the recalculation of tariff rates is not possible, then the *TE* of customs valuation procedures can be calculated as follows. Let P_v be the value placed on imports by the valuation procedure and P_f, as above, be the f.o.b. free-market price. Then

$$TE^{VAL} = \frac{P_v}{P_c} t - t \qquad \text{(VIII.B)}$$

Note that only the excess of the actual ad valorem incidence of the tariff over the announced tariff rate t is regarded as an NTB, since the tariff t is already included in the measure of the country's tariff protection.

C. Valuation procedures become true NTBs when they are not well-defined, so that importers do not know until they reach the border what the duty will be. The trade restricting impact of such uncertainty is difficult to determine, but in cases where it is clear that such an impact exists, it should somehow be accounted for. One way would simply be to increase the value of the tariff arbitrarily, as in the above formula. Alternatively one could try to infer from other prices how much extra is being charged in this market to compensate for the uncertainty. Thus if the producing firm sells the product also in another export market that is subject neither to this uncertainty nor to other

NTBs, or if it sells the product in its own domestic market, then the formulas given above for TE^{EXP} or TE^{OWN} can be used. The analogue to the quota rent in the discussion there of quotas allocated to foreigners is not here a rent at all, but rather a compensation for uncertainty.

IX. Technical Barriers to Trade

Technical barriers to trade are regulatory and certification mechanisms that are designed in a way that puts imports at a disadvantage relative to domestic goods. Like customs valuation procedures, these have been limited by agreements under both the Tokyo and Uruguay Rounds of trade negotiations. Nonetheless, new needs for regulation and certification are constantly arising, and the possibility that these will be handled in discriminatory ways will continue to exist. Unfortunately, they are one of the most difficult NTBs imaginable to quantify. Our only general suggestion, aside from trying to extract credible assessments of their costs from experts in the affected industries, is again to use the formulas given above for TE^{EXP} or TE^{OWN} for quantifying quotas based on comparisons with other export markets or with the own domestic market of the exporter.

For a specific technical barrier that is thought to exist in a specific industry, the best approach is to collect information from experts in the industry itself. What information is needed depends somewhat on the nature of the barrier. As noted in the text, technical standards, regulations, and certification requirements can constitute barriers to trade in several different ways:

A. If more stringent standards are applied to imported as compared to domestically produced goods, then one must determine how much more costly it is to satisfy those more stringent standards. Letting the (per unit) cost of satisfying domestic standards be denoted C_{StandD} and the cost of satisfying the standard on imports be C_{StandM}, the tariff equivalent of the standards is

$$TE^{STAND1} = \frac{C_{StandM} - C_{StandD}}{P_c} \qquad \text{(IX.A)}$$

B. If identical regulations are enforced more stringently on imports than on domestic goods, then of course one needs to compare the costs to the two groups of producers of satisfying the standards. If these costs are identifiably different, then the formula for TE^{STAND1} can be used directly. Alternatively, if the measurable difference is in the fractions of product units that are made to satisfy a single standard at a cost of C_{Stand}, then letting θ_D and θ_M be the fractions of output satisfying the standard, we have

$$TE^{STAND2} = \frac{(\theta_M - \theta_D)\, C_{Stand}}{P_c} \qquad \text{(IX.B)}$$

C. Finally, if imports are subjected to more costly certification procedures than domestically produced goods, then TE^{STAND1} can again be used directly but with the two costs measuring costs of certification rather than of satisfying the standards.

X. Domestic Subsidies

As illustrated in Figure 3.3 and discussed in Chapter 3, domestic subsidies can affect trade, but not in a way that is equivalent to a tariff in terms of its effect on prices. Therefore we cannot usefully define a tariff equivalent of a domestic subsidy. Nonetheless, the measure of subsidies is important, and we recommend that a separate measure be used for them, the Output Subsidy Equivalent, OSE. It is defined as the ongoing cash payment, per unit of output and as a percent of cost, that would be equivalent to the actual subsidy in terms of its effect on output. Thus, an actual cash subsidy to output is just measured as a percent of cost. Similarly, for a subsidy to variable inputs (inputs of which more is needed to produce more output), one should calculate the OSE as the cost reduction per unit of output, but since the cost reduction is just the subsidy itself, this too is the subsidy as percent of cost.

More difficult are subsidies that do not appear to be related to output. For example, an ongoing cash payment to a firm that is truly unrelated to its outputs or its inputs does not change the amount the firm will supply to the market at prices for which it would have covered costs even without the subsidy. But at lower prices, at which the firm would have shut down and supplied nothing, the OSE is either the excess of cost over price or the subsidy payment divided by output, whichever is smaller. Thus the OSE of such a subsidy depends upon the prevailing price in the market, being zero for prices above cost and positive for prices below cost. Whether to use long run average cost, LAC, or short run average variable cost, VAC, for these purposes depends on the circumstances. If the subsidy is paid every year indefinitely, thus permitting the firm to survive in the long run, then LAC is the appropriate cost measure. However, if the subsidy is temporary, then it matters for output in the short run only if price is below VAC, so that the firm would otherwise have stopped producing.

What then of a one-time subsidy that is unrelated to current or future output?[4] Such a subsidy is equivalent to a permanent interest-free loan, and thus to an ongoing payment each year of the one-time subsidy times the interest rate. However, because this benefit is received regardless of whether the firm produces or not, it has no effect on output and its OSE is zero.

We summarize and elaborate these suggestions in the formulas below, using the following notation:

S = Total subsidy payments per unit time

S_0 = One-time subsidy payment

Q = Output per unit time

C_a = Long-run average cost per unit output

C_v = Short-run variable cost per unit output

P_{av} = Average ex-factory price over time

A. If subsidies are paid directly for output, or if they are paid for inputs that vary with output, then

$$OSE^{OUT} = \frac{S}{C_a Q} \qquad \text{(X.A)}$$

B. If an ongoing subsidy per unit time is paid independently of the size of output as long as output is positive, then

$$OSE^{IND1} = \begin{cases} 0 & \text{if } P_{av} > C_a \\ \min\left(C_a - P_{av}, \dfrac{S}{C_a Q}\right) & \text{if } P_{av} < C_a \end{cases} \qquad \text{(X.B)}$$

C. If a temporary subsidy per unit time is paid independently of the size of output as long as output is positive, then for the periods in which the subsidy is paid (with P_e the ex-factory price in the period),

$$OSE^{IND2} = \begin{cases} 0 & \text{if } P_e > C_v \\ \min\left(C_v - P_e, \dfrac{S}{C_v Q}\right) & \text{if } P_e < C_v \end{cases} \qquad \text{(X.C)}$$

D. If a one-time subsidy is paid that is related to output, such as a capital subsidy, then the amount of the subsidy should be converted to an equivalent ongoing flow using the real interest rate, i:

$$OSE^{OUT0} = \frac{iS_0}{C_a Q} \qquad \text{(X.D)}$$

E. If a one-time subsidy is not related to output, then its OSE is zero:

$$OSE^{IND0} = 0 \qquad \text{(X.E)}$$

Notes

1. Most countries report tariffs as percent of the c.i.f. price. For the few other countries, such as the United States, that instead report relative to the f.o.b. price, this and all other formulas in this appendix should be multiplied by P_c/P_f, which in most cases just means replacing P_c with P_f.

2. See, for example, Moroz and Brown (1987, Table D2).

3. Greenaway et al. (1995) employ an econometric method to quantify the trade-reducing effects of potential ADDs, but their method does not always succeed, even for them, and we do not regard it as a generally applicable methodology.

4. A subsidy to expanding capital *is* related to output and can be dealt with as above. It should be converted from a stock to a flow, however, by multiplying by the interest rate. See (X.D) below.

APPENDIX 4

Measurement of Barriers to Trade in Services and Foreign Direct Investment

Given the fact that international trade in services has been increasing significantly in recent decades and now is equal to about 20 percent of global merchandise trade, it is obviously important to consider the barriers that affect services trade and issues of measurement of these barriers. There has been similarly an increasing amount of foreign direct investment (FDI) in both goods and services sectors in and between advanced and developing countries. This also is subject to a variety of barriers and thus merits attention.

Characteristics and Modes of International Transactions in Services

The most distinguishing characteristic of services transactions is that their production and consumption occur simultaneously, thus often requiring direct contact between producers and consumers. While some services are traded internationally across borders (e.g., "separated" services such as telecommunications) in a manner similar to cross-border trade in goods, other services may require the consumer to move to the location of the producer, as in the case of tourism. Further, because of the necessary proximity of consumers and producers, factors of production may have to move across national boundaries to the place of consumption. Thus FDI may be necessary in order to establish a foreign commercial presence, and there may also be temporary cross-border movement of labor that is required to serve foreign consumers.

Barriers to Trade in Services

As noted by Hoekman and Primo Braga (1997, p. 288), because of the simultaneity of the production and consumption of services, border measures such as tariffs will generally be difficult to apply because customs agents cannot readily observe the service as it crosses the border. Typically therefore the restrictive policies followed will be designed to limit the access of foreign services and the suppliers of services to domestic markets. Hoekman and Primo Braga distinguish the following types of barriers: (1) quotas, local content, and prohibitions; (2) price-based instruments; (3) standards, licensing, and procurement; and (4) discriminatory access to distribution networks.

Quantitative-restriction (QR) type policies are commonly applied to service providers. Two prominent examples are the bilateral agreements regulating international air transportation services, which are usually reciprocal and company specific, and ocean-cargo-sharing arrangements, which also often rely on reciprocity in providing shipping services in mutual trade. In many countries, there are outright prohibitions directed against foreign providers of such services as domestic transportation, basic telecommunications, and legal, insurance, education, surveying, and investment advising services. Restrictions on transborder data flows are also prevalent and may impede market access by foreign providers.

Price-based instruments may take the form of visa fees and entry or exit taxes, discriminatory airline landing fees, and port taxes. Tariffs can be significant barriers to trade in goods that embody services (e.g., films, television programs, computer software) or goods that are used in producing services (e.g., computers, telecommunications equipment, advertising material). Further, many service sectors are subject to government-sanctioned or monitored price controls, examples including air transportation, financial services, and telecommunications. Government subsidies are commonly used in such service sectors as construction, communications, and road and rail transport.

Licensing or certification requirements may be imposed on foreign providers of professional and business services. Environmental standards may also impact on service providers, particularly in transportation and tourism. Government procurement policies are often designed to favor domestic over foreign providers of services as well as goods by means of preference margins and outright prohibitions.

Discriminatory access to distribution and communications systems exists in many countries in such sectors as telecommunications, air transport, advertising, insurance, and dealer networks.

Measurement of Barriers to Trade in Services

The measurement of services barriers parallels to an extent our treatment of the measurement of NTBs that limit trade in goods. However, services barriers involve greater complexities when account is taken of the different modes of supply of services that include not only cross-border trade but also the movement of consumers to the location of providers as well as FDI and temporary international movement of labor.

Frequency measures of barriers to services trade have been constructed by PECC (1995) and Hoekman (1996). These are based on the information contained in the country schedules of the General Agreement on Trade in Services (GATS) and refer to all four modes of the supply of services. Frequency ratios are constructed based on the number of commitments scheduled in the GATS by individual countries that designate sectors or sub-sectors unrestricted or partially restrictive in relation to the maximum possible number of unrestricted commitments. As noted in Hoekman (1996, p. 101), there are 155 sectors and sub-sectors and four modes of supply, which yields 620×2=1,440 total commitments on market access and national treatment for each of 97 countries.[1]

Hoekman (1995) has used frequency ratios to approximate the relative degree of restrictiveness of market-access barriers to services trade across countries and sectors. He established a judgmental set of benchmark tariff equivalents for individual sectors to reflect the degree to which market access to these sectors was restricted. The benchmark tariff equivalents chosen ranged from a high of 200 percent for sectors (e.g., maritime cabotage, air transport, postal services, voice telecommunications, and life insurance) in which market access was essentially prohibited in most countries to 20-50 percent for sectors in which market access was less constrained. He then assigned a value to each country and sector using the benchmarks multiplied by the calculated frequency ratio. Thus, for example, assuming a benchmark tariff equivalent of 200, say, for postal services and a frequency ratio of 50 percent to reflect the scheduled market access commitments, the tariff equivalent for that sector is set at 100 percent. Using the value of output by sector for a representative industrialized country, it is then possible to construct weighted average measures by sector and country. The weighted average tariff equivalents for 1-digit ISIC sectors for selected countries are indicated in Table A.4.1.

It should be emphasized that Hoekman's measures are designed to indicate the *relative* degree of restriction and are not to be taken literally as indicators of absolute ad valorem tariff equivalents. But even granting this, there are some important limitations worth mentioning. Thus, as Hardin and Holmes (1997, p. 72) note, Hoekman's method may be misleading or biased because it assumes that the absence of positive country commitments in the GATS schedules can be interpreted as indicating the presence of restrictions, which may in fact not be the case. Also, the different types of restrictions are given equal weight and are not distinguished according to their economic impact. Finally, market access restrictions are the only ones taken into account.

It should be evident from the foregoing discussion that there is a need to devise more direct and precise methods for measuring the barriers to trade in services. The available frequency-type measures are useful in identifying the types of barriers and the relative degree of protection afforded to particular sectors. But, as we pointed out in our earlier discussion, frequency-type measures have only limited economic content with regard to assessing the size of service barriers and the consequences of maintaining or eliminating these barriers.[2] Much remains to be done therefore, especially to develop price-based measures of services restrictions that can be used to assess the costs and the benefits from their reduction or elimination.[3]

Barriers to Foreign Direct Investment (FDI)

Hardin and Holmes (1997, p. 32) define an FDI barrier as

> "...any government policy measure which distorts decisions about where to invest and in what form. ...policy measures such as limits on the level of foreign investment, or the need to go through costly and time-consuming screening processes to convince authorities that FDI in a project will be in the national interest, are considered barriers."

In considering ways of classifying FDI barriers, Hardin and Holmes note (pp. 33-34):

> "The appropriate classification system may vary, depending on the purpose of the exercise. For example, if the purpose is to check and monitor compliance with some policy commitment, then the categories should reflect the key element of the commitment.... If the primary interest is instead the resource allocation implications of the barriers, some additional or different information may be useful.
>
> Barriers to FDI may distort international patterns and modes of...trade. They may also distort allocation of capital between different economies, between foreign and domestic investment, between different sectors, and between portfolio and direct investment. ...the classification system...should highlight the key characteristics of the barriers that will determine their size and impact. Market access and national treatment are...relevant categories from a resource allocation perspective. ...national treatment is generally taken to refer to measures affecting firms after establishment. A...way to classify barriers is therefore...according to what aspect of the investment they most affect: establishment, ownership and control; or operations. In addition..., some further information may be useful...on distinctions...between direct versus indirect restrictions on foreign controlled firms; and rules versus case-by-case decisions."[4]

The main types of FDI barriers that have been identified by UNCTAD (1996) are noted in Table 4.A.2. Further information on the barriers most commonly used to restrict FDI especially in the APEC economies is provided in Hardin and Holmes (1997, esp. pp. 37-40 and 45-55). As they note (p. 40), some common characteristics appear to be:[5]

> "application of some form of screening or registration process involving various degrees of burden for the foreign in-

vestor; restrictions on the level or share of foreign ownership, particularly in some service sectors, and often in the context of privatisations; widespread use of case-by-case judgments, often based on national interest criteria; widespread use of restrictions on ownership and control (e.g., restrictions on board membership), particularly in sectors such as telecommunications, broadcasting, banking; and relatively limited use of performance requirements on input controls in services sectors."

Measurement of Barriers to FDI

Many of the issues already discussed regarding the measurement of barriers to merchandise trade have their analogue in measurement of barriers to FDI. Thus, as Hardin and Holmes (1997, p. 59) note, restrictions on foreign ownership are similar to quotas on imports of goods. Consider Figure 4.A.1, which is the case of a small country facing a perfectly elastic world supply of capital at R_w and with the demand and supply schedules for domestic capital, D and S. If there are no restrictions, the equilibrium capital inflow will be Q_dQ_t. If now the share of foreign capital is limited to 25 percent, the demand schedule will shift to D_2, and, in the new equilibrium, the capital inflow will be $Q_{dr}Q_{tr}$ and the rate of return will increase to R_r. The implicit tariff on foreign investment will be $R_r - R_w$. There is a tax on users of capital equal to $R_r$bdD_w, which is transferred in part to domestic suppliers of capital who now receive higher returns, $R_r$acR_w. The area abcd is analogous to a quota rent and can be captured by foreign investors or by government if the rights are auctioned. If the world supply schedule of capital were upward sloping, foreign suppliers would face lower returns and thus bear part of the tax equivalent of the investment restriction. It will be evident that the tariff equivalent on imported capital will vary depending on the elasticity of the demand and supply schedules and the substitutability between domestic and foreign capital.[6] This, together with differences in regulatory regimes, will make it difficult to undertake intercountry comparisons of tariff equivalents for FDI restrictions.

Indirect restrictions on FDI (e.g., screening, local content requirements) will increase the costs of and lower the returns to FDI. This is illustrated in Figure 4.A.2. The initial equilibrium is R_w and Q_1. A barrier will shift the domestic supply schedule from S_1 to S_2, with a new equilibrium at Q_2. The domestic rate of return rises to R_u and the foreign rate of return falls to R_i. The tariff equivalent will be R_iR_u.

The preceding examples illustrate that the measurement of barriers to FDI will depend on whether the barriers are direct and will affect asset prices or rates of return or whether the barriers are indirect and will affect the costs of providing the good or service and thereby result in lower rates of return. As a practical matter, it would appear to be rather difficult to isolate these different effects.

As was discussed above in the case of services, it is possible to construct frequency and coverage ratios for barriers to FDI. But as Hardin and Holmes (1997, p. 71) note, these measures provide no information about the likely impacts that barriers to FDI may have on rates of return or prices. Hardin and Holmes attempt accordingly to build on and improve Hoekman's methodology for constructing guesstimates of tariff equivalents for services. In particular, they use information on actual FDI restrictions and incorporate information on the types of barriers and their economic impact. Their objective is to construct an index of FDI restrictions that can be translated into a tariff equivalent or tax equivalent.

The components of their proposed index and the weights assigned to the different sub-categories are given in Table A.4.3. They set the weights to reflect the relative degree of restriction of different barriers. Foreign equity limits are given greater weights than the other barriers noted. Hardin and Holmes confine their calculations of the indexes of FDI restrictions to the services sectors in the APEC countries.[7] They find (p. 77) that communications and financial services are most subject to FDI restrictions, while business, distribution, environmental, and recreational services are the least restricted.[8]

While the indexes of FDI restrictions are useful in identifying the relative restrictiveness of measures applied in particular sectors and countries, they are still essentially judgmental in character. It would be desirable accordingly to focus attention on the ways in which the different types of FDI restrictions affect rates of return and/or prices and to construct data measures that can be used in analyzing the economic effects involved.[9]

TABLE A.4.1. Constructed Ad Valorem Tariff Equivalent "Guesstimates" by 1-Digit ISIC Services Sectors for Selected Countries (Percentage)

Country	ISIC 5 Construction	ISIC 6 Wholesale & Retail Distr.	ISIC 7 Transp., Storage & Communic.	ISIC 8 Business & Fin. Services	ISIC 9 Social & Personal Services
Australia	12.0	7.4	183.4	24.8	25.4
Austria	5.0	4.6	98.7	20.1	13.9
Canada	6.0	9.0	117.7	25.9	40.2
Chile	40.0	34.4	182.2	45.2	42.9
European Union	10.0	10.0	182.0	27.2	23.6
Finland	19.0	14.6	181.0	23.8	31.7
Hong Kong	32.0	31.5	149.8	39.0	42.9
Japan	5.0	4.6	142.0	28.9	32.3
Korea	16.0	21.4	164.9	36.3	40.7
Mexico	24.0	21.3	152.3	40.9	29.8

New Zealand	5.0	13.4	181.5	30.5	36.1
Norway	5.0	13.4	122.2	25.7	24.0
Singapore	12.0	34.4	138.8	35.9	33.7
Sweden	12.0	13.4	184.2	22.5	26.9
Switzerland	5.0	8.0	178.1	27.7	32.3
Turkey	5.0	34.4	31.6	35.4	35.9
United States	5.0	4.6	111.4	21.7	31.7

Source: Hoekman (1995, pp. 355-56).

TABLE A.4.2. Barriers to FDI

Restrictions on market entry	Bans on foreign investment in certain sectors
	Quantitative restrictions (e.g., limit of 25 per cent foreign ownership in a sector)
	Screening and approval (sometimes involving national interest or net economic benefits tests)
	Restrictions on the legal form of the foreign entity
	Minimum capital requirements
	Conditions on subsequent investment
	Conditions on location
	Admission taxes
Ownership and control restrictions	Compulsory joint ventures with domestic investors
	Limits on the number of foreign board members
	Government appointed board members
	Government approval required for certain decisions
	Restrictions on foreign shareholders' rights
	Mandatory transfer of some ownership to locals within a specified time (e.g., 15 years)
Operational restrictions	Performance requirements (e.g., export requirements)
	Local content restrictions
	Restrictions on imports of labor, capital and raw materials
	Operational permits or licences
	Ceilings on royalties
	Restrictions on repatriation of capital and profits

Source: UNCTAD (1996).

TABLE A.4.3. Components of an Index of FDI Restrictions

Type of restriction	Weight
Foreign equity limits on all firms	
no foreign equity permitted	0.5
less than 50 per cent foreign equity permitted	0.5
more than 50 per cent and less than 100 per cent foreign equity permitted	0.25
Foreign equity limits on existing firms, none on greenfield	
no foreign equity permitted	0.5
less than 50 per cent foreign equity permitted	0.25
more than 50 per cent and less than 100 per cent foreign equity permitted	0.125
Screening and approval	
investor required to demonstrate net economic benefits	0.1
approval unless contrary to national interest	0.075
notification (pre or post)	0.05
Control and management restrictions	
all firms	0.2
existing firms, none for greenfield	0.1
Input and operational restrictions	
all firms	0.2
existing firms, none for greenfield	0.1

Source: Hardin and Holmes (1997, p. 76). Copyright © 1997 Commonwealth of Australia; reprinted with permission.

FIGURE A.4.1. The Impact of a Limit on the Share of Foreign Ownership

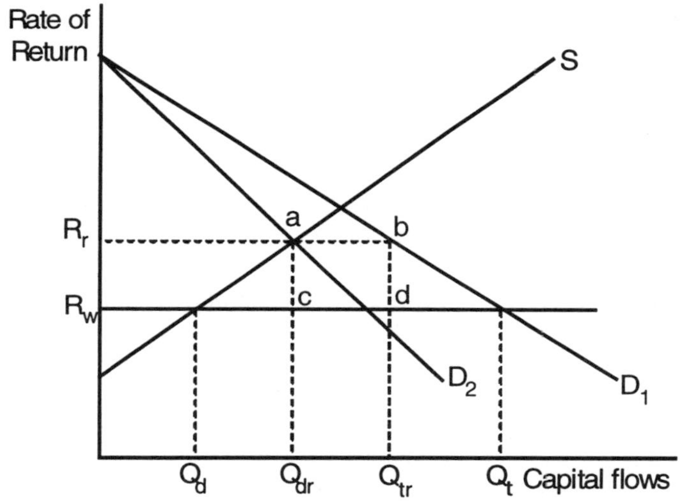

Source: Hardin and Holmes (1997, p. 61). Copyright © 1997 Commonwealth of Australia; reprinted with permission.

FIGURE A.4.2. The Impact of an FDI Restriction that Increases the Cost of the Investment

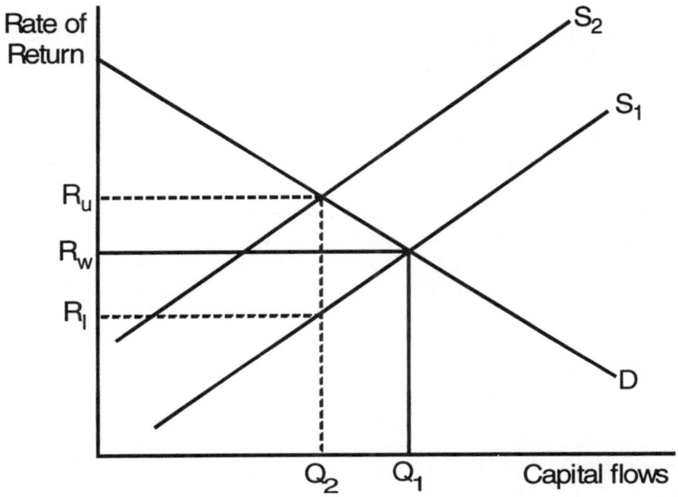

Source: Hardin and Holmes (1997, p. 67). Copyright © 1997 Commonwealth of Australia; reprinted with permission.

Notes

1. As noted in Hardin and Holmes (1997, p. 70) the GATS commitments are based on a "positive list" approach and therefore do not take into account sectors and restrictions which are unscheduled. In PECC (1995), it is assumed that all unscheduled sectors and commitments are unrestricted, which will then significantly lower the calculated frequency ratios. It would be useful accordingly to determine how accurate the PECC assumption may be.

2. See Brown, Deardorff, Fox, and Stern for an illustrative computable general equilibrium (CGE) analysis of the potential impacts of services trade liberalization using Hoekman's ad valorem tariff guesstimates. They find that the effects of partially liberalizing services trade are of the same order of magnitude as the liberalization of industrial products in the Uruguay Round.

3. See, for example, Francois et al. (1996) for price wedges that can be attributed to the Jones Act that restricts U.S. trade in domestic water transportation (cabotage) services. They estimate that removal of the Jones Act would increase U.S. economic welfare by $2.0-$3.4 billion annually, using observed 1989 real consumption as the base for evaluating the change involved.

4. Direct restrictions include limitations on the total size or share of investment in a sector and requirements on inputs used (e.g., local content). Indirect restrictions include net benefit or national interest criteria and limitations on membership of company boards. The distinction between rules and case-by-case decisions relates to issues of clarity in specification and transparency as compared to the exercise of administrative discretion.

5. Hardin and Holmes (pp. 40-43) also provide information on investment incentives, which are widely used and for the most part are not subject to multilateral disciplines.

6. The fact that services may be provided in a variety of modes complicates the analysis. That is, a limitation on FDI in a new enterprise may cause firms to switch to other more costly modes of supply. Complications also arise from limitations on FDI in an existing enterprise, which will affect asset prices on rates of return.

7. Details on the construction of the indexes and their sensitivity to variations in the restrictive weights are discussed in Hardin and Holmes (1997, esp. 103-11).

8. Sectoral and country results are given in Hardin and Holmes (1997, pp. 77-81 and 112-117).

9. Petri (1997) has constructed a CGE model framework that is designed explicitly to examine the economic effects of the liberalization of both trade and FDI. In the absence of direct measures of existing barriers to FDI, Petri (p. 26) models barriers to FDI as a tax on capital income, that is, a quota premium that is returned to households and does not absorb productive resources. The rates chosen for the primary and manufacturing sectors are based on the tariff equivalents for these tradable sectors that are available in the 1992 GTAP data base. The rates for the services sectors are based on the tariff equivalents of barriers to market access for the four modes of services constructed by Hoekman (1995) and used by Brown et al. (1996) in analyzing the potential economic effects of the liberalization of services barriers. Petri applies his model to the liberalization of trade and FDI barriers in the APEC economies. He concludes that such liberalization would increase real expenditure by $260 billion (on a 1992 base), and that about 40 percent of this increase would stem from FDI liberalization. The potential benefit from the liberalization of FDI barriers thus appears substantial. More precise measurement of these barriers would certainly be helpful accordingly to pin down more accurately the size of the benefits from FDI liberalization and the region/country and sectoral effects involved.

Name Index

Subject Index

STUDIES IN INTERNATIONAL TRADE POLICY

Studies in International Trade Policy includes works dealing with the theory, empirical analysis, political, economic, legal relations, and evaluations of international trade policies and institutions.

General Editor: Robert M. Stern

John H. Jackson and Edwin Vermulst, Editors. *Antidumping Law and Practice: A Comparative Study*

John Whalley, Editor. *Developing Countries and the Global Trading System.* Volumes 1 and 2

John Whalley, Coordinator. *The Uruguay Round and Beyond: The Final Report from the Ford Foundation Project on Developing Countries and the Global Trading System*

John S. Odell and Thomas D. Willett, Editors. *International Trade Policies: Gains from Exchange between Economics and Political Science*

Ulrich Kohli. *Technology, Duality, and Foreign Trade: The GNP Function Approach to Modeling Imports and Exports*

Stephen V. Marks and Keith E. Maskus, Editors. *The Economics and Politics of World Sugar Policies*

J. Michael Finger, Editor. *Antidumping: How It Works and Who Gets Hurt*

Horst Herberg and Ngo Van Long, Editors. *Trade, Welfare, and Economic Policies: Essays in Honor of Murray C. Kemp*

David Schwartzman. *The Japanese Television Cartel: A Study Based on* Matsushita v. Zenith

Alan V. Deardorff and Robert M. Stern, Editors. *Analytical Perspectives and Negotiating Issues in the Global Trading System*

Edwin Vermulst, Paul Waer, and Jacques Bourgeois, Editors. *Rules of Origin in International Trade: A Comparative Study*

Alan V. Deardorff and Robert M. Stern, Editors. *The Stolper-Samuelson Theorem: A Golden Jubilee*

Kent Albert Jones. *Export Restraint and the New Protectionism: The Political Economy of Discriminatory Trade Restrictions*

Alan V. Deardorff, James A. Levinsohn, and Robert M. Stern, Editors. *New Directions in Trade Theory*

Robert Baldwin, Tain-Jy Chen, and Douglas Nelson. *Political Economy of U.S.–Taiwan Trade*

Bernard M. Hoekman and Petros C. Mavroidis, Editors. *Law and Policy in Public Purchasing: The WTO Agreement on Government Procurement*

Danny M. Leipziger, Editor. *Lessons from East Asia*

Tamin Bayoumi. *Financial Integration and Real Activity*

Harry P. Bowen, Abraham Hollander, and Jean-Marie Viaene. *Applied International Trade Analysis*